Learn Italian with Gina and Other Stories

HypLern Interlinear Project
www.hyplern.com

First edition: 2025, July

Author: Emilio de Marchi
Translation: Kees van den End
Foreword: Camilo Andrés Bonilla Carvajal PhD

ISBN: 978-1-989643-34-1

kees@hyplern.com
www.hyplern.com

Learn Italian with Gina and Other Stories

Interlinear Italian to English

Author
Emilio de Marchi

Translation
Kees van den End

HypLern Interlinear Project
www.hyplern.com

The HypLern Method

Learning a foreign language should not mean leafing through page after page in a bilingual dictionary until one's fingertips begin to hurt. Quite the contrary, through everyday language use, friendly reading, and direct exposure to the language we can get well on our way towards mastery of the vocabulary and grammar needed to read native texts. In this manner, learners can be successful in the foreign language without too much study of grammar paradigms or rules. Indeed, Seneca expresses in his sixth epistle that "Longum iter est per praecepta, breve et efficax per exempla[1]."

The HypLern series constitutes an effort to provide a highly effective tool for experiential foreign language learning. Those who are genuinely interested in utilizing original literary works to learn a foreign language do not have to use conventional graded texts or adapted versions for novice readers. The former only distort the actual essence of literary works, while the latter are highly reduced in vocabulary and relevant content. This collection aims to bring the lively experience of reading stories as directly told by their very authors to foreign language learners.

Most excited adult language learners will at some point seek their teachers' guidance on the process of learning to read in the foreign language rather than seeking out external opinions. However, both teachers and learners lack a general reading technique or strategy. Oftentimes, students undertake the reading task equipped with nothing more than a bilingual dictionary, a grammar book, and lots of courage. These efforts often end in frustration as the student builds mis-constructed nonsensical sentences after many hours spent on an aimless translation drill.

Consequently, we have decided to develop this series of interlinear translations intended to afford a comprehensive edition of unabridged texts. These texts are presented as they were originally written with no changes in word choice or order. As a result, we have a translated piece conveying the true meaning under every word from the original work. Our readers receive then two books in just one volume: the original version and its translation.

The reading task is no longer a laborious exercise of patiently decoding unclear and seemingly complex paragraphs. What's more, reading becomes an enjoyable and meaningful process of cultural, philosophical and linguistic learning. Independent learners can then acquire expressions and vocabulary while understanding pragmatic and socio-cultural dimensions of the target language by reading in it rather than reading about it.

Our proposal, however, does not claim to be a novelty. Interlinear translation is as old as the Spanish tongue, e.g. "glosses of [Saint] Emilianus", interlinear bibles in Old German, and of course James Hamilton's work in the 1800s. About the latter, we remind the readers, that as a revolutionary freethinker he promoted the publication of Greco-Roman classic works and further pieces in diverse languages. His effort, such as ours, sought to lighten the exhausting task of looking words up in large glossaries as an educational practice: "if there is any thing which fills reflecting men with melancholy and regret, it is the waste of mortal time, parental money, and puerile happiness, in the present method of pursuing Latin and Greek[2]".

Additionally, another influential figure in the same line of thought as Hamilton was John Locke. Locke was also the philosopher and translator of the Fabulae AEsopi in an interlinear plan. In 1600, he was already suggesting that interlinear texts, everyday communication, and use of the target language could be the most appropriate ways to achieve language learning:

> ...the true and genuine Way, and that which I would propose, not only as the easiest and best, wherein a Child might, without pains or Chiding, get a Language which others are wont to be whipt for at School six or seven Years together...[3]

---

1 "The journey is long through precepts, but brief and effective through examples". Seneca, Lucius Annaeus. (1961) Ad Lucilium Epistulae Morales, vol. I. London: W. Heinemann.

2 In: Hamilton, James (1829?) History, principles, practice and results of the Hamiltonian system, with answers to the Edinburgh and Westminster reviews; A lecture delivered at Liverpool; and instructions for the use of the books published on the system. Londres: W. Aylott and Co., 8, Pater Noster Row. p. 29.

3 In: Locke, John. (1693) Some thoughts concerning education. Londres: A. and J. Churchill. pp. 196-7.

Who can benefit from this edition?

We identify three kinds of readers, namely, those who take this work as a search tool, those who want to learn a language by reading authentic materials, and those attempting to read writers in their original language. The HypLern collection constitutes a very effective instrument for all of them.

1. For the first target audience, this edition represents a search tool to connect their mother tongue with that of the writer's. Therefore, they have the opportunity to read over an original literary work in an enriching and certain manner.
2. For the second group, reading every word or idiomatic expression in its actual context of use will yield a strong association between the form, the collocation, and the context. This will have a direct impact on long term learning of passive vocabulary, gradually building genuine reading ability in the original language. This book is an ideal companion not only to independent learners but also to those who take lessons with a teacher. At the same time, the continuous feeling of achievement produced during the process of reading original authors both stimulates and empowers the learner to study[1].
3. Finally, the third kind of reader will notice the same benefits as the previous ones. The proximity of a word and its translation in our interlinear texts is a step further from other collections, such as the Loeb Classical Library. Although their works might be considered the most famous in this genre, the presentation of texts on opposite pages hinders the immediate link between words and their semantic equivalence in our native tongue (or one we have a strong mastery of).

---

1 Some further ways of using the present work include:

1. As you progress through the stories, focus less on the lower line (the English translation). Instead, try to read through the upper line, staying in the foreign language as long as possible.
2. Even if you find glosses or explanatory footnotes about the mechanics of the language, you should make your own hypotheses on word formation and syntactical functions in a sentence. Feel confident about inferring your own language rules and test them progressively. You can also take notes concerning those idiomatic expressions or special language usage that calls your attention for later study.
3. As soon as you finish each text, check the reading in the original version (with no interlinear or parallel translation). This will fulfil the main goal of this

collection: bridging the gap between readers and original literary works, training them to read directly and independently.

Why interlinear?

Conventionally speaking, tiresome reading in tricky and exhausting circumstances has been the common definition of learning by texts. This collection offers a friendly reading format where the language is not a stumbling block anymore. Contrastively, our collection presents a language as a vehicle through which readers can attain and understand their authors' written ideas.

While learning to read, most people are urged to use the dictionary and distinguish words from multiple entries. We help readers skip this step by providing the proper translation based on the surrounding context. In so doing, readers have the chance to invest energy and time in understanding the text and learning vocabulary; they read quickly and easily like a skilled horseman cantering through a book.

Thereby we stress the fact that our proposal is not new at all. Others have tried the same before, coming up with evident and substantial outcomes. Certainly, we are not pioneers in designing interlinear texts. Nonetheless, we are nowadays the only, and doubtless, the best, in providing you with interlinear foreign language texts.

Handling instructions

Using this book is very easy. Each text should be read at least three times in order to explore the whole potential of the method. The first phase is devoted to comparing words in the foreign language to those in the mother tongue. This is to say, the upper line is contrasted to the lower line as the following example shows:

--Credo di no, --ella rispose stentatamente.
(I) believe ~~of~~ not she answered haltingly

The second phase of reading focuses on capturing the meaning and sense of the original text. As readers gain practice with the method, they should be able to focus on the target language without getting distracted by the translation. New users of the method, however, may find it helpful to cover the translated lines with a piece of paper as illustrated in the image below. Subsequently, they try to understand the meaning of every word, phrase, and entire sentences in the target language itself, drawing on the translation only when necessary. In this phase, the reader should resist the temptation to look at the translation for every word. In doing so, they will find that they are able to understand a good portion of the text by reading directly in the target language, without the crutch of the translation. This is the skill we are looking to train: the ability to read and understand native materials and enjoy them as native speakers do, that being, directly in the original language.

--Credo di no, --ella rispose stentatamente.
(I) believe ~~of~~ not

In the final phase, readers will be able to understand the meaning of the text when reading it without additional help. There may be some less common words and phrases which have not cemented themselves yet in the reader's brain, but the majority of the story should not pose any problems. If desired, the reader can use an SRS or some other memorization method to learning these straggling words.

--Credo di no, --ella rispose stentatamente.

Above all, readers will not have to look every word up in a dictionary to read a text in the foreign language. This otherwise wasted time will be spent concentrating on their principal interest. These new readers will tackle authentic texts while learning their vocabulary and expressions to use in further communicative (written or oral) situations. This book is just one work from an overall series with the same purpose. It really helps those who are afraid of having "poor vocabulary" to feel confident about reading directly in the language. To all of them and to all of you, welcome to the amazing experience of living a foreign language!

Additional tools

Check out shop.hyplern.com or contact us at info@hyplern.com for free mp3s (if available) and free empty (untranslated) versions of the eBooks that we have on offer.

For some of the older eBooks and paperbacks we have Windows, iOS and Android apps available that, next to the interlinear format, allow for a pop-up format, where hovering over a word or clicking on it gives you its meaning. The apps also have any mp3s, if available, and integrated vocabulary practice.

Visit the site hyplern.com for the same functionality online. This is where we will be working non-stop to make all our material available in multiple formats, including audio where available, and vocabulary practice.

Table of Contents

Storia Di Una Gallina
The Story of a Chicken

STORIA DI UNA GALLINA
Story   of   a   hen

Vìvevano   una volta   due vecchi sposi.   Egli   non
Lived   one time   two   old   spouses   He   not
There lived   once   an old couple

si   chiamava   Taddeo,   ma   Paolino,   ed   essa,
himself   named   Taddeus   but   Paolino   and   that one
                      (christian saint)   she

la   signora Brigida, buone anime entrambe.   Il   sor
the   lady   Brigida   good   souls   both (of them) The   Mr.

Paolino   lavorava   in   canestri   e   la   moglie   in
Paolino   worked   in   baskets   and   the   wife   in
                                weaving

raggiustare   le   calze;   dopo   trent'anni,   si
adjusting   the   stockings   after   thirty years   each other
(mending)

volevano   bene   come   il   primo   giorno   di
wanted   well   like   the   first   day   of
(they wished)

matrimonio,   anzi,   invecchiando,   miglioravano
marriage   even   aging   improving
                              (as they aged)

nell'amore, come il vino nelle botti suggellate. Se
in the love / like / the / wine / in the / barrels / sealed / If

il Cielo mi concedesse tanto buon tempo che io
the / Heaven / me / conceded / such / (a) good / time / that / I

potessi raccontare giorno per giorno la vita del
could / tell / day / by / day / the / life / of the

sor Paolino, e della sora Brigida, crederei di
Mr. / Paulino / and / of the / Mrs. / Brigida / (I) would believe / of

giovare col mio libro a' miei simili, ben
to be good for / with -the- / my / book / to / my / fellow men / well

più che con un trattato di meccanica celeste:
more / that / with / a / treatise / of / mechanics / celestic
(than) / / / / / about astronomy

perchè, dopo tutto, l'amore e la benevolenza
because / after / all / the love / and / the / benevolence

sono il pernio, sul quale la ruota del mondo
are / the / pivot / on the / which / the / wheel / of the / world
/ / {perno}

gira senza stridere. Ma poichè questa
turns / without / screeching / But / then-that / this
/ / (squeaking) / / (since)

consolazione non mi è concessa dalle circostanze,
consolation / not / me / is / conceded / by the / circumstances

racconterò almeno in quest'occasione del santo
(I) will tell / at least / in / this occasion / of the / saintly

Natale un episodio della loro vita, che farà
Christmas / an / episode / of -the- / their / life / that / will make

piangere, io credo, tutte le anime sensibili. Beato
cry / I / believe / all / the / souls / sensitive / Blessed

chi piange, e una lagrima, dice un libro chinese,
who / cries / and / a / tear / says / a / book / Chinese

è più grande del mare.
is / more / large / of the / sea
/ / / (than the)

Dopo l'esperienza fatta negli anni passati e
After / the experience / made / in the / years / passed / and
/ / (they had)

sempre in loro danno, i nostri buoni
always / in / their / damage / -the- / our / good
/ (to) / (disadvantage)

vecchietti eran venuti entrambi del parere di
old ones / were / come / both / of the / opinion / of
/ (had)

allevare in casa una gallinetta, per vederla crescere
to raise   in   house   a   little hen   for   to see it   grow

sotto i loro sguardi all'avvicinarsi di queste
under -the- their   watch   at the approaching itself   of   these

ultime feste dell'anno, togliendo così il pericolo,
last   feasts   of the year   removing   like that   the   danger

tanto comune oggidì, di dover mangiare una
so much   common   today   of   to have to   eat   one

cosa per l'altra o fors'anche una porcheria.
thing   for   the other   or   maybe also   a   piece of crap
    (instead of)

E poichè sono sull'argomento, si sa oggimai
And   then-that   (I) am   on the argument   one   knows   today
   (since)   (on the subject)

che, se tutte le lepri, che si mangiano
that   if   all   the   hares   that   -themselves-   (people) eat
                              are eaten

all'osteria potessero parlare, i topi non
at the tavern   could   speak   the   mice   not

starebbero a sentirle; come, per altra parte,
would stay   to   hear them   like   for   other   part

accade spesso a qualcuno, mentre siede col
happens often to someone while (he) sits with -the-

suo pezzo di manzo sul piatto, di vederselo
his piece of beef on the plate of to see himself it

scappar via al suono d'una frustata. La lepre
escape away at the sound of a whip The hare
(hare-meat)

è gatto, il bue è cavallo, e così via il vino
is cat the ox is horse and like that away the wine
(cat-meat)

è aceto, l'aceto è veleno; non c'è speranza
is vinegar the vinegar is poison not there is hope

che nel tempo, quando, cioè, le cose saranno
that in the time when that is the things will be
(will have)

diventate così naturalmente false, che per
become like that naturally false that for

cambiare torneranno quelle di prima. Ma intanto
to change turn (into) those of before But meanwhile

i nostri vecchietti, giunti sulla sessantina,
-the- our old ones together on the sixties
(in their)

dovevano per obbligo di coscienza guardarsi
had to for oblige of conscience to guard themselves

dalle cose false e tener da conto lo stomaco:
from the things false and to have of check the stomach
(in)

non meritano lode, se al'avvicinarsi delle feste
not (they) deserve praise if at the approaching of the feasts

comperavano una gallinetta viva per nutrirla
(they) bought a little hen lively for to feed it

colle loro mani?
with -the- their hands

La cara bestiola passeggiava per casa da
The dear beast strolled about (the) house since

circa tre mesi, chiocciando, piluccando, ruspando,
about three months clucking pecking scratching

come fanno tutte le sue pari. Brigida, mentre
like do all -the- its peers Brigida while

suo marito stava alla bottega, soleva discorrere
her husband was at the shop used to talk

con lei o le tagliuzzava foglie di verze, o le
with her or her cut leaves of cabbage or her

sbriciolava del pan di melica, invitandola a
crumbled -of the- bread of melic (grass) inviting to

bere in una terrina bianca che pareva porcellana.
drink in a bowl white that seemed porcelain

Che dirò del sor Paolino? prima d'entrare
What will (I) say of the Mr. Paolina before of to enter (entering)

si fermava dietro l'uscio chiamando chi-chi-chi;
himself stopped behind the door calling chi-chi-chi

se fosse stata nelle nuvole, la povera bestia
(even) if (she) was been in the clouds the poor beast
(she had)

correva giù. Il canestrajo allora rovesciava le
ran down The basket weaver then turned over the

tasche in terra e ne usciva del grano,
pockets in ground and of it came out -of the- grain
(on the)

del pane, del biscotto, che la gallina
-of the- bread -of the- biscuit that the hen

bezzicava divinamente sotto gli occhi beati dei
devoured / divinely / under / the / eyes / blissful / of -the-

suoi padroni. Una vedova che abitava vicino al
her / masters / A / widow / that / lived / close / to -the-

loro uscio e che, dopo la morte d'un suo
their / door / and / that / after / the / death / of one / her

pappagallo non poteva resistere a tali spettacoli,
parrot / not / seemed / to resist / -to- / such / shows

piangeva come una bambina.
cried / like / a / child

--Che peccato! --disse un giorno il sor Paolino,
What sin (a shame) / said / one / day / -the- / Mr. / Paolino

--che peccato che la povera bestia non possa
what sin (a shame) / that / the / poor / animal / not / can

assaggiare una goccia del mio caffè! oggi ha
taste / a / drop / of -the- / my / coffee / today / (it) has

mangiato asciutto e le farà peso.
eaten / dry / and / it / will make / weight

La sora Brigida invece trovava che, stando sempre
The Mrs. Brigida instead found that standing always

in cucina sul mattone, avrebbe patito
in (the) kitchen on the brick (she) would have suffered

del freddo; non che volesse dire con ciò
from the cold not that (she) wanted to say with that

che un paio di calzette sarebbero convenute a una
that a pair of socks would be convenient to a

gallina, ma fece in modo che Paolino stendesse
hen but (she) did in manner that Paolino extended
            she made sure   (stretched)

almeno una vecchia stuoja presso l'acquaio. E
at least an old mat close to the sink And

bisogna dire che la gallina avesse veramente
(it is) necessary to say that the hen had truly

dei meriti, perchè con niente non si fa il
-of the- merits because with nothing not itself makes the

buon brodo, nè la buona stima. Le penne infatti
good broth nor the good esteem The feathers in fact
(soup)

le aveva screziate sul petto e d'un bel colore
her had striped on the breast and of a pretty color
(she)

rosso dorato sulla schiena; le zampe magre e
red golden on the back the paws thin and

svelte, l'occhio vivace e malizioso la sua parte,
quick the eye lively and mischievous the its part
(each)

e ai ragionamenti dei padroni rispondeva con
and at the reasoning of the masters (she) answered with

certi movimenti del collo, degni di qualunque
certain movements of the neck worthy of any

ragazza da marito. Le volevano bene, dunque,
girl of husband Her (they) wanted well then
(for) (they wished)

non solo perchè fosse una gallina, ma perchè gli
not only because (she) was a hen but also the

animi buoni si attaccano volentieri alle
spirits good themselves attached willingly to the

cose buone. Mentre i due vecchietti sedevano a
things good While the two old ones sat at

tavola   a   mangiare quel po' di carne comechessia,
(the) table to   eat   that bit of meat like-that-(it)-is

comperata   dal   beccaio (nè potevano allevarsi in
   bought   from the barn   nor could (they) raise itself in

casa   un   bue   come   un   pulcino),   la   gallinetta
house   an   ox   like   a   chicklet   the   chick

saltava   su,   guardava   ne'   piatti,   ora   coll'occhio
jumped   up   looked   in the   plates   now   with the eye

destro,   ora   col   sinistro,   con   tanta   innocenza
right   now with the   left   with so much   innocence

che   i   due   vecchietti   perdevano   la   memoria
that the two   old ones   lost   the   memory

dell'appetito.
 of the appetite

Ma   i   giorni   passano   per   tutti.   Già   si
But   the   days   pass   for   everyone   Already   one

discorreva   delle   feste,   come   se   fossero   giunte:
talked about -of- the feasts   as   if   (they) were   arrived
                                      (they had)

la gente pensava al modo di passarle bene
the people thought at the manner of to pass them well

e il Natale veniva innanzi colle sue scarpe
and the Christmas came onwards with -the- her shoes

di feltro.
of felt

I nostri due buoni vecchietti già da cinque
The our two good old people already since five

o sei giorni si vedevano sopra pensiero,
or six days themselves saw on thought (the mind)

come se avessero nel capo un cespuglio di spine;
as if (they) had in the head a bush of thorns

ma, essendo e l'uno e l'altra d'indole timida
but being and the one and the other of nature shy

e rispettosa, per paura di farsi torto
and respectful for fear of to make themselves wronged

a vicenda, masticavano in silenzio il loro dolore.
to another chewed in silence -the- their pain

La gioja comune che si spande in questi giorni
The joy commune that itself spreads in these days

e che rischiara le case e gli animi della
and that brightens the houses and the spirits of the

gente, non li rallegrava, anzi se qualcuno diceva:
people not them rejoiced even if someone said

--buone feste, sora Brigida, --essa rispondeva
good feasts Mrs. Brigida that one responded
happy holidays (she)

appena, crollando malinconicamente la testa.
hardly slumping melancholically the head

Anche il sor Paolino a bottega non era
Also the Mr. Paolino at (the) workshop not was

più lui; stava immobile, colle mani sul
(any)more himself (he) stood still with the hands on the

canestro, gli occhi fissi in terra e pensava: --Se
basket the eyes fixed in ground and thought If
on the ground

non fosse che la Brigida ha bisogno d'un vitto
not (it) was that the Brigida has need of a food

sano   e   nutriente, chi oserebbe strappare una
healthy   and   nutritious   who   would dare   to take   a

penna   a   quella povera creatura?
feather   at   that   poor   creature
      (from)

E   la   sora Brigida   dal   canto suo, correndo
And   the   Mrs.   Brigida   from the   part   hers   running

sulla   calza: --Se quel pover'uomo non avesse   lo
on the   sock   If   that   poor man   not   had   the

stomaco disfatto, se non avesse speso per allevarla,
stomach   unmade   if   not   (he) had   spent   for   to raise it
      (unwell)

chi   avrebbe   cuore?...   ma   dirà   che   sono
who   would have   (the) heart   but   (he) will say   that   (they) are

tenerezze   da   donna   malata,   e   riderà   di me;
tendernesses   of   (a) woman   sick   and   (he) will laugh   of   me

come noi   ci   burliamo della nostra vicina.
like   we   ourselves   laugh   of -the-   our   neighbor

Così   passò   qualche   altro   giorno,   senza   che
Like that   passed   some   other   day   without   that

nè   l'uno   nè   l'altra   osasser   toccare   quel   brutto
neither   the one   nor   the other   dare   touch   that   ugly

tasto.
touch
(subject)

Mancavano   tre   giorni   appena   al   Natale   e
Lacked   three   days   hardly   to -the-   Christmas   and
(It was still)

bisognava   uscirne.   Sedevano   entrambi   innanzi
(they) needed   to get out of it   (They) sat   together   in front

al   camino,   dopo   un   pranzo   di   magro   fatto   con
to the   fireplace   after   a   lunch   -of-   meager   made   with

certi   pesci,   che   forse   non   eran   pesci.   Egli,   il   sor
certain   fish   that   maybe   not   were   fish   He   the   Mr.

Paolino,   andava   costruendo   colle   molle   una
Paolino   went   building   with the   fire tongs   a

catasta   di   fuscellini,   intorno   a   un   ceppo,   che
stack   of   twigs   around   -at-   a   log   that

bruciava   vivo   vivo,   ed   essa,   la   sora   Brigida,   in
burned   lively   lively   and   that one   the   Mrs.   Brigida   in
                            (she)

una cuffia di traliccio, colle mani sotto il
a cap of trellis with the hands under the

grembiule, piangeva in silenzio nell'ombra.
apron cried in silence in the shadow

--Credi tu, amor mio, --cominciò il sor
Believe you love (of) mine began the Mr.

Paolino, --che fosse veramente una tinca che
Paolino that (it) was really a tench that

abbiamo mangiato?
(we) have eaten

--Credo di no, --ella rispose stentatamente.
(I) believe -of- not she answered haltingly

--Se si potesse tenerli in casa nella
If oneself could have them in (the) house in the

catinella i pesci, come si tengono i
basin the fishes like themselves (they) keep the

polli nella stia, si potrebbe vedere,
chickens in the sty one could see

--soggiungeva il marito per tirare il discorso
added   the husband to pull the discourse

sull'argomento.
on the argument

Brigida si scosse sulla sua sedia e soffocò
Brigida herself shook on -the- her seat and stifled

un sospiro dentro di sè per non dare segno a
a sigh   inside of herself for not to give sign to

quel pover'uomo della sua sciocca debolezza.
that poor man of -the- her silly weakness

Vedeva troppo bene che Paolino contava di poter
(She) saw too   well that Paolino told   of to be able

mangiare almeno il giorno di Natale qualche
eat   at least the day   of Christmas some

cosa di schiettamente sano.
thing of   plain   health

--Essa non immagina punto il mio pensiero,
That one not imagined point -the- (of) my thought
(She)   (understands) (nothing)

--disse fra sè il buon uomo, a cui
said between himself the good man to whom
(inside)

spiaceva e come uomo e come marito di
was sorry and as mand and as husband of

mostrarsi in qualche parte da meno di sua
to show himself in some part of (at) least of his

moglie. Sedevano innanzi al fuoco, come
wife (The) sat in front of -to- the fire like

dicevo, scaldandosi le ginocchia e discorrendo
(he) said scalding himself the knee and talking

così, quando a un tratto videro venire
like that when at a stretch (she) saw come
all of a sudden

innanzi la loro gallina, che si era levata
towards (him) -the- their hen that herself was raised

ad ora insolita, e che veniva a specchiarsi
at the hour unusual and that come to mirror herself
(be reflected)

nella fiamma. Le sue penne mandavano bagliori
in the flame The her feathers sent flashes

e fosforescenze d'oro e di piropo e, o fosse
and phosphorescence of gold and of pyrope and or was

che i poveri vecchi la vedessero attraverso le
that the poor old ones her saw through the

lagrime, o fosse altrimenti, parve loro una cosa
tears or was otherwise seemed to them a thing

piovuta dal Cielo, se non proprio il gallo
rained (down) from the Sky if not itself the rooster

che convertì San Pietro.
that converted Saint Peter

Il sor Paolino non potè resistere a quella vista,
The Mr. Paolino not could resist at that sight

e con un pretesto uscì; e uscita anch'essa,
and with a pretext went out and went out also she

poco dopo, la povera donna, andò a bussare
little after the poor woman went to knock

all'uscio della vedova, in cerca d'un consiglio. Il
at the door of the widow in search of an advice The

canestraio trovò per via Angiolino del Trapano,
basket maker found by way Angiolino of the Trapano

suo vecchio amico, uomo prudente e quasi
his old friend man prudent and almost

letterato, gerente d'un giornale politico, che
literate manager of a magazine political that

propugnava una santa causa, Angiolino ascoltò la
advocated a holy cause Angiolino listened to the

gran passione dell'amico e si concertarono
great passion of the friend and themselves agreed

insieme sul modo di regolarsi in questa difficile
together on the manner of to settle in this difficult

circostanza.
circumstance

La mattina dopo, e precisamente la vigilia di
The morning after and precisely the eve of

Natale, Angiolino venne a trovarlo a casa e
Christmas Angiolino came to find him to (the) house and

strinse la mano alla sora Brigida. Egli s'era
squeezed the hand to the Mrs. Brigida He himself was
(shook) (of the)

messo quel dì l'abito scuro e teneva in mano il
put (on) that day the suit dark and had in hand the

cappello a cilindro come soleva fare nelle
hat and cylinder like (he) used to do in the

cerimonie o nei processi contro la santa causa.
ceremonies or in the processes against the holy cause

Parlò della mala piega delle cose d'Europa, dei
(He) spoke of the bad twist of the things of Europe of the

tempi che si fanno grossi, della poca fede, della
times that itself made large of the little faith of the

poca umanità che c'è nel mondo, e stava per
little humanity that there is in the world and stood for

aprire la bocca sull'argomento (che già Paolino
to open the mouth on the argument that already Paolino

era sugli spilli), quando entrò dall'altra parte
was on the pins when (he) entered of the other side

anche la vedova, cogli occhi rossi, come il
also the widow with the eyes red like the

giorno che aveva trovato il suo pappagallo
day that (she) had found -the- her parrot

strozzato fra due ferri della gabbia. Era
choked between two bars of the cage (It) was

anche questa un'intelligenza presa fra le due
also this an intelligence taken between the two

donne. Tutti e quattro sedettero, sconcertati
women All -and- four sat down disconcerted

ciascuno per riguardo agli altri, mentre la gallina,
each one for regards of the others while the hen

più fortunata di tutti, passeggiava tranquilla,
more fortunate of all passed calm
(than)

beccando le screpolature, quasi che al mondo
pecking the cracks almost that at the world

non esistessero nè i grandi nè i piccoli affanni.
not existed nor in big nor in small cares

Vi   fu un istante di silenzio.
There was   a   moment of   silence

Poi   Angiolino del Trapano, carezzando   colla
Then   Angiolino del   Trapano   caressing   with the

manica il pelo del   suo cappello, coll'occhio
sleeve   the hair on -the- his   head   with the eye

fisso alla gallina: --Fortunate le galline, --disse,
fixed at the hen   Fortunate (are) the chickens (he) said

che sfuggono   a   queste preoccupazioni! Esse
that   escape   from   these   worries   These

posseggono ancora quella semplicità che gli
possess   still   that   simplicity   that the

uomini,   fatti tiranni di sè stessi, mettono in
men   (who) made tyrants of one selves   put   in

non cale, correndo dietro, come sciacalli, al
no   care   running   after like jackals -to the-

proprio interesse, paghi soltanto quando sono
their own interests paying   only   when   (they) are

pagati. Beati i tempi dei patriarchi, quando gli
paid Blessed the times of the patriarchs when the

uomini si contentavano d'un piatto di
men themselves satisfied of a platter of
(with a)

lenticchie, nè avevano bisogno, come si vede in
lentils nor had need as one sees in

questi giorni, d'insanguinarsi le mani nella strage
these days of to bloody the hands in the massacres

di tante creature, che sono pure creature di Dio!
of so many creatures that are also creatures of God

Quanto più bello e santo sarebbe,
How much more beautiful and saintly (it) would be

specialmente in queste occasioni, mostrar la
especially in these occasions to show the
{Christmas}

bontà dell'animo nostro, concedendo riposo e
goodness of the spirit ours conceding repose and

tregua anche agli animali vivi e morti, che sono
respite also to the animals alive and dead that are
(have)

stati creati non per l'ingordigia umana, ma per
been created not for the greed human but for

far più lieta la natura col loro canto
to make more joyful -the- nature with -the- their song

armonioso, collo splendore delle loro piume,
harmonious with the splendor of -the- their plumes

col tenero belato, col guizzar rapido e
with the tender bleating with the flicker rapid and

snello nelle acque dei fiumi. L'usignolo col
slender in the waters of the streams The nightingale with -the-

suo canto notturno... --seguitava Angiolino del
its song nocturnal continued Angiolino of the

Trapano; ma uno scoppio di pianto interruppe il
Trapano but a burst of tears interrupted the

bel discorso. Paolino strinse nelle sue la mano
beautiful speech Paolino squeezed in the his the hand

della Brigida, e sorridendo sotto il velo delle
of -the- Brigida and smiling under the veil of the

lagrime, esclamò:
tears   exclaimed

--Noi non saremo tanto cattivi; anch'essa mangerà
We   not   will be   so   bad   also that one will eat

nel   nostro piattello.
in -the- our   plate
(from)

Quelle   care   persone   si   accordarono   di
Those   dear   persons   themselves   agreed   of

pranzare insieme il giorno di Natale, per far
to lunch together the   day   of Christmas for to make

più lieta la festa dell'umanità. La sora Brigida
more happy the feast of the humanity The Mrs. Brigida

preparò un   pranzetto d'uova, di   berlingozzi,
prepared a   little lunch of egg of   Berliners
                                      (donuts)

d'insalata, e un pasticcio di riso e, poichè i
of salad and a   pasty of rice and since the

tempi sono diventati così tristi, che uno non sa
times are become so sad that one not knows

ormai quel che compera e quel che mangia a
almost that what (one) buys and that what (one) eats at

tavola, aggiunse per riguardo agli ospiti, anche
(the) table added out of respect to the guests also

una gallina delle solite, comperata sul mercato,
a hen of the usual bought on the market

la mattina al buio, senza discutere, sicura in
the morning at the dark without to discuss sure in
          (in the)

cuor suo che questa almeno non sarebbe stata
heart (of) her that this at least not would be been
                                      (would have)

una gallina.
a hen

Gina

Gina

GINA Man mano che il Natale, col suo
Gina   Hand   (by) hand   that   -the-   Christmas   with -the-   her
While gradually

regalo di neve, si avvicinava, si facevano
gift   of   snow   herself   approached   themselves   made

sempre più spaventosi i rimorsi di quella
always   more   fearful   the   remorses   of   that

ragazza: perchè la sua mamma poveretta, era
girl   because   -the-   her   mamma   poor   was
poor mamma   (had)

morta appunto una mattina di Natale, mentre la
died   exactly   one   morning   of   Christmas   while   the

Gina non toccava ancora i nove anni, e il
Gina   not   touched   yet   -the-   nine   years   and   the
(reached)

pensiero della mamma, anche in mezzo alle
thought   of the   mamma   also   in   (the) middle   to the

più sciocche vanità della vita, aveva sempre
most foolish vanities of -the- life had always

conservato per la giovane un certo qual profumo,
conserved for the youth a certain some fragrance

come di fiori d'altare. Oggi, passati molti
like of flowers of altar Today (having) passed many

anni da quel giorno, la Gina aveva abbandonata
years from that day -the- Gina had abandoned

la casa paterna, per venire a cercar fortuna in
the house paternal for to live to search fortune in

città. Giunta a Milano col canestrino di fiori,
(the) city Arrived at Milan with the little basket of flowers

perchè era bella, se l'erano
because (she) was beautiful themselves her were
(her had)

messi d'attorno i giovinotti e uno fra' tanti
put of arround the young men and one between many
surrounded

che l'aveva tentata, pareva che le volesse bene;
that her had tried seemed that her wanted well

così almeno egli giurava sempre, toccandosi
like that   at least   he   swore   always   touching himself

colla mano il posto del cuore. E veramente,
with the   hand   the   place   of the   heart   And   truly

ne' primi tempi, fu per la Gina una specie
in the   first   times   (it) was   for   -the-   Gina   a   sort

di sogno. La stagione era viva, la città allegra e
of   dream   The   season   was   alive   the   city   happy   and

piena di gente, gli amici cortesi; per cui ella
full   of   people   the   friends   courteously   for   who   she

potè facilmente guadagnarsi un appartamento tutto
could   easily   earn herself   an   appartment   all

per lei, con specchi, dorature, cortine di seta,
for   herself   with   mirrors   gildings   curtains   of   silk

e un gabinetto chinese con una specchiera, che
and   a   cabinet   chinese   with   a   dressing table   that

pareva un reliquiario. E dire che la Gina alla
seemed   a   reliquary   And   to say   that   -the-   Gina   at the
        (holder of relics)

Ghiacciata   s'era   lavata   il   viso   le   dodici volte
Ghiacciata   herself was washed the face -the- twelve times
              (had)

nel   secchio! ma   fortuna   e   dormi,   dice   il
in the bucket   but   fortune   and   sleep   says   the

proverbio,   ossia   chi   bella   nasce   ha   la   dote
proverb   or that who beautiful is born has the dowry

nelle fasce.   I   fotografi   amavano   ritrarla   in
in the wraps The photographers loved   to portray her in

grande,   per   farne   dei   quadri   agli   angoli
large   for   to make of it of the paintings at the corners

delle   vie: un   cappellino,   portato   dalla   Gina,
of the streets a   little hat   brought from the   Gina
                                            (by the)

poco   mancava   che   diventasse   subito   di   moda
little   lacked   that   turned   immediately of fashion

e   se   le   signore   --quell'altre--   non   andavan
and   if   the   ladies   those others   not   went

dietro   al   modello,   gli   era   soltanto   per   non
after   -to- the model   it   was   only   for   not

dimostrare che la Gina fosse più bella di
to demonstrate that -the- Gina was more beautiful of
(than)

loro. Tuttavia anche sotto quella cipria, anche in
them Yet even under that powder even in

mezzo alla spuma frizzante di quella vita,
(the) middle to the froth sparkling of that life
(of the) sparkling froth

fra le garze e i nastri color di rosa, la
between the gauze and the ribbons color of pink -the-

Gina provava nel cuore una specie di puntura,
Gina felt in the heart a kind of prick

come se una spina vi si fosse rotta dentro;
as if a thorn there itself was broken inside

e in fondo ai cartocci pieni di cose dolci,
and in bottom at the boxes filled of things sweet
(with)

che le regalavano a teatro, sentiva sempre un
that her (they) gave at (the) theater (she) felt always a

amaro di legno quassio, perchè il peccato non
bitterness of wood quamo because the sin not
quamo wood

si sputa fuori, nè tutte le macchie si
itself spits out nor all the stains themselves

lavano col sapone. Anzi, quanto più pareva
wash with the soap Indeed when more (it) seemed

che il suo occhio di gazzella fosse talvolta
that -the- her eye of gazelle was sometimes

rapito in una apoteosi dell'opera, e in una
rapt in a apotheosis of the opera and in a

contraddanza di driadi ed amadriadi, tanto più
quadrille of dryads and amadryads so much more

il suo pensiero sprofondava nelle fessure della
-the- her thought(s) sank into the cracks of the

coscienza e le accadeva di vedere, fra le
consciousness and her happened of to see between the

piante della scena, spuntare un campanile aguzzo,
plants of the scene to sprout a bell tower pointed

colla crocetta in cima, o la siepe dove soleva
with the cross in (the) top or the hedge where (she) used

curare le oche, o il pergolato e il
to take care (of) the geese or the pergola and the

ballatoio di legno, coll'insegna della Ghiacciata, la
gallery of wood with the sign of -the- Ghiacciata the

famosa osteria del suo babbo.
famous tavern of -the- her father

Fanciulletta vi era cresciuta, a piedi nudi, col
Girl there was grown at feet bare with the

bel musetto sporco, coi capelli in furia, cogli
pretty little face dirty with the hairs in fury with the (tangles)

occhi neri e lustri come il carbone, amata
eyes black and shiny like the coal loved

prima dalla sua mamma, odiata poi dalla
first by -the- her mother hated then by the

matrigna, che aveva una ragazza brutta e storta.
stepmother that had a girl ugly and crooked

Quando la matrigna aveva gente, la Gina
When the stepmother had people (guests) -the- Gina

scappava di sopra, apriva un guardaroba, ne
escaped -of- up opened a wardrobe of it

toglieva una veste lunga, per il gusto d'indossarla
took out a dress long for the pleasure of to wear it

e di fare la coda sull'ammattonato,
and of to make the tail on the brick floor

passeggiando innanzi allo specchio con una
passing in front to the mirror with a

ventola in mano, di penne di tacchino. La
fan in hand from feathers of turkey The

matrigna ne la pagava poi con sferzate di vero
stepmother for it her paid after with lashings of real

legno di nocciuolo, o con schiaffi per il gusto
wood of nut and with slaps for the taste

che avrebbe voluto anch'essa di voltarle la faccia.
that (she) had wanted also that one of to turn her the face
(also she)

Ma la faccia della Gina si faceva sempre più
But the face of -the- Gina itself made always more

bella, come se le ceffate finissero d'aggiustarla:
beautiful like if the slaps finished of to fix it
{ceffone}

gli occhi, spesse volte lagrimosi, acquistavano una
the eyes often times tearful acquired a

profondità infinita, come chi guardasse nell'acqua
depth infinite like who guards in the water

del mare, e così spuntò la primavera dei
of the sea and like that appeared the spring of -the-

suoi sedici anni. All'osteria della Ghiacciata, che
her seventeen years At the tavern of the Ghiacciata that

aveva d'intorno un bel boschetto di carpini
had of around a pretty grove of hornbeam (tree)
was situated in

e di sambuco, venivano al primo aprirsi
and of elderberry came at the first opening itself

della primavera, molte comitive in carrozza, di
of the spring many groups in carriage of

giovani e di donne bellissime, che dopo il
youths and of women very beautiful that after the

pranzo si mettevano a ballare sul battuto.
lunch themselves set to dance on the beat

Il Toppa, un cretino dalla gola gonfia e dagli
The Toppa a fool of the (with the) throat swollen and of the (with the)

occhi malati, suonava l'organetto per muovere
eyes sick sounded (played) the little organ for to move

certe scarpette di seta, che il diavolo, io credo,
some fine shoes of silk that the devil I believe

suggerisce ai parigini per far perdere la
suggests to the Parisians for to make loose the

strada alle anime innocenti. Anche la Gina
way to the souls innocent Also -the- Gina

imparò a ballare, cioè quando ci si provò la
learned to dance that is when it herself (she) tried the

prima volta, si meravigliò essa stessa di
first time herself surprised that one (her) self of

saperlo fare. È vero che essa aveva ballato
to know it do And really that that one had danced

molte volte ne' suoi sogni, quando, a quindici
many times in -the- her dreams when at fifteen

anni non si dorme inutilmente; ma tutti dicevano
years not one sleeps uselessly but all said

che danzava di scuola, e che pareva di
that (she) danced of school and that (she) seemed of
(from)

portare una piuma, se si appoggiava al
to wear a feather if herself (she) leaned at the

braccio del cavaliere.
arm of the cavalier
(nobleman)

Imparò anche a far dei mazzolini e vide in
(She) learned also to make of the bouquets and saw in

seguito che i fiori stavano bene in un canestro
following that the flowers stood well in a basket
(looked)

di vimini. Una volta che una di quelle signore
of wicker One time that one of those ladies

dimenticò un cappello di paglia, a foggia di
forgot a hat of straw at shape of
(with)

paniere, colla tesa larga e piovente, la Gina
(a) basket with the brim wide and raining -the- Gina
(turned up)

se lo provò sul capo, e vide che pareva
herself it tried on the head and saw that seemed

anch'essa un fiore nel paniere. Ci pensò
also that one a flower in the basket (Of) it (she) thought
(also she)

un poco; ogni mattina, da un pezzo in qua,
a bit one morning from a bit in here

soleva correre incontro al procaccia, per
used to run to meet with at the courier for

togliergli di mano un biglietto ricamato con una
to take of him of hand a card embroidered with a

corona di conte, Ci pensò un pezzo, finchè
crown of count (Of) it (she) thought a bit until

una volta che la matrigna osò buttarle il
one time that the stepmother dared to throw her the

cencio dei piatti sul muso, non disse nulla,
rag of the dishes on the face not (she) said nothing

ma scrisse due righe sopra un foglio. Due
but wrote two lines on a piece of paper Two

giorni dopo, col pretesto che andava in chiesa
days after with the pretext that (she) went in church

a messa, nel suo scialletto nero, prese la
to mass in the her shawl black (she) took the

strada postale, camminò nella polvere e sotto il
street postale walked in the dust and under the
(main)

sole per un bel tratto, finchè giunta allo
sun for a good stretch until that (she) arrived at the

svolto, dov'era una gran siepe di robinie,
turn where was a large hedge of locust (tree)

scoperse una carrozza. Il cuore fe' sulle prime
discovered a carriage The heart made at the first

un gran schiamazzo, che non facevano l'eguale le
a great shout that not made the same -the-

sue dieci oche nei giorni di temporale; sostò,
her ten geese in the days of storm (she) paused

41

chiuse gli occhi un minuto, e quando li
closed the eyes a minute and when them

riaprì, credette quasi che l'aria fosse
(she) reopened (she) believed almost that the air was

infocata, Qualcuno la spingeva bel bello: una
inflamed Someone her pushed pretty pretty a
(burning)

voce sussurrava al suo orecchio; la carrozza
voice whispered at the her ear the carriage
(in)

fece il resto.
did the rest

Dopo tre mesi di vita gaja, la Gina ammalò
After three months of life gay -the- Gina fell ill

di tifo: e se non era una vecchierella di
of typhus and if not (there) was an old woman of
(with)

buon cuore che si pose a curarla, presso il
good heart that herself set to cure her by the

guanciale, gli amici l'avrebbero lasciata morire
pillow her friends her would have let die

come un cane, nel suo bel gabinetto chinese.
like a dog in -the- her pretty cabinet chinese

Quando potè cacciare le gambe dal letto
When (she) could stick out the legs from the bed

e si guardò nello specchio trovò che,
and herself watched in the mirror (she) found that

meno gli occhi, molto di bello se n'era
apart from the eyes much of beauty itself of her was

andato: i capelli se li sentì pochi nelle
gone the hairs themselves they felt little in the

mani, non così però che con un po' di
hands not like that however that with a bit of

belletto, e con qualche truciolo finto ella non
makeup and with some shaving fake she not

potesse sperare di vincere ancora la sua
could hope of to conquer still -the- her

fortuna. Uscì per le strade a vender fiori,
fortune (She) exited for the streets to sell flowers

ma visto che la gente non credeva più alla
but seen that the people not believed (any)more at the
(in the)

Gina di prima, pensò al modo di diventare
Gina of before (she) thought at the manner of to become

un'altra Gina, poveretta! La vecchia signora, che
an other Gina (the) poor girl The old lady that

l'aveva curata con tanto amore, le offrì ricovero
her had cured with so much love her offered shelter

in casa sua, in una viuzza tranquilla e fuor di
in house (of) her in an alley quiet and out of

mano, dove il sole non scendeva un momento,
hand where the sun not went down a moment
(the way)

che per scappar via. Passò l'estate. L'autunno
that for to escape way Passed the summer The autumn

venne innanzi col suo tabarrotto di nebbia:
came onwards with -the- its cloak of fog

venne anch'esso il dicembre nella sua pelliccia
came also that -the- december with the its fur

d'ermellino, e lassù intanto, in quelle quattro
of ermine / and / up there / meanwhile / in / those / four

stanze, colava l'aria fredda, livida, inzuppata dì
rooms / dripped in / the air / cold / livid / soaked / of (in)

malinconia. Quando la Gina sentiva qualche cosa
melancholy / When / -the- / Gina / felt / some / thing

alla gola, che minacciava di strozzarla, usciva
at the / throat / that / threatened / -of- / to strangle her / (she) exited

in cerca di sole, rubando cogli occhi l'ultimo
in / search / of / sun / stealing / with the / eyes / the last

verde, che spenzolava dai rami degli alberi.
green / that / dangled / from the / branches / of the / trees

Si avvicinava il Natale, l'anniversario della
Itself / approached / -the- / Christmas / the anniversary / of -the-

sua povera mamma. Il profumo del lauro, la
her / poor / mamma / The / perfume / of the / laurel / the

vista del muschio, degli aranci, dei presepi,
view / of the / moss / of the / oranges / of the / nativity scenes

dei balocchi di legno verniciati, esposti nelle
of the — toys — of — wood — painted — displayed — in the

botteghe e sui banchini, risuscitavano una folla
shops — and — on the — stalls — revived — a — crowd

di reminiscenze, un polverìo, come sopra una
of — memories — a — dust cloud — like — on — a

strada pesta da cavalli sfrenati. La Gina se
street — beaten — by — horses — unrestrained (wild) — The — Gina — herself

ne tornava a casa, colla febbre nelle ossa,
of it — turned — to — (the) house — with the — fever — in the — bone(s)

colle guance riarse, con una gran sete: si
with the — cheeks — parched — with — a — great — thirst — herself

accoccolava per terra, sotto la finestra, al
(she) crouched — by (on the) — ground — under — the — window — at the

buio, o cogli occhi incantati sui fiocchi di
dark — and — with the — eyes — enchanted — on the — flakes — of

neve che cadevano; nelle ore di notte che non
snow — that — fell — in the — hours — of — night — that — not

poteva dormire, o che dormiva così a sbalzi,
(she) could sleep or that (she) slept like that at jolts

coll'animo sospeso e co' piedi freddi, essa
with the soul suspended and with the feet cold that one (she)

si lasciava andare a ripensare le belle carte
herself let go to rethink the beautiful cards

di torrone, che.... una volta il babbo le regalava,
of nougat that one time the dad her gave

delle quali ne aveva un fascio in una scatola,
of the which of it (she) had a bundle in a box

quali screziate d'oro e d'argento, quali con
those speckles of gold and of silver those with

bei lembi color cielo, color vestito della
beautiful strips color (of the) sky color (of the) dress of the

Madonna, altre gentili come le perle, altre
Madonna other lovely like -the- pearls others

accese come il fuoco; e ne faceva vesti alle
lit like the fire and of it (she) made vests to the

sue bambole di carta, alla Ghiacciata, se ne
her dolls of paper to the Ghiacciata if of it

ornava ella stessa le orecchie, tagliuzzando le
adorned she herself the ears cutting off the

laminette di paglia d'oro, tintinnanti; quasi il
blades of straw of gold rustling almost the

destino avesse dovuto prepararle, per i suoi
future had had to to prepare her for the her

begli occhi, una corona di diamanti, come a una
beautiful eyes a crown of diamonds like to a

principessa.... Così pensava fredda fredda
princess Like that (she) thought cold cold
(she was thinking)

nel letto.
in the bed

Ahimè! la corona l'aveva avuta sul capo, non
Alas the crown it (she) had had on the head not

importa se di gemme false. L'acqua era scesa
(it) mattered if of gems false The water was fallen down

per la sua china, trascinandola verso il mare;
by the its slope dragging her towards the sea

ma che mare! meglio il pantano, ove andavano
but the sea better the quagmire where went

guazzando le sue oche nei tempi di secco.
waddling -the- her geese in the times of drought

Se ne sentiva sudicia l'anima e la bocca. Non
Herself of it (she) felt dirty the spirit and the mouth Not

pareva più il suo corpo, tanto le vesti
(it) seemed (any) more -the- her body so much the dresses

le scappavano giù e i capelli si
her escaped down and the hairs themselves

irritavano sul capo come lische. E intanto
irritated on the head like fishbones And meanwhile

correva per le vie il santo Natale, caro ai
ran by the roads the holy Christmas dear to the

bambini, a suon di piva, circondato il capo
children at sound of bagpipes {from Italy} surrounded (crowned) the head

d'edera   e   di   muschio;   ogni   masserizia   era
of ivy   and   of   moss   each   furnishing   was
{piece of household}

pulita   e   benedetta: ogni   piedino   aveva   le   sue
clean   and   blessed   each   leg   had   the   her

calzette   di   lana,   bianche   o   a   liste   di   colore;
socks   of   wool   white   or   at   strips   of   colors
(with)

s'imbandivano   le   mense   accanto   al   fuoco,   dove
themselves were set   the   tables   besides   the   fire   where

bruciava   il   lauro,   spandendo   un   profumo   di
burned   the   laurel   spreading   a   perfume   of

presepio   e   di   Betlemme.   V'era   della   gente
nativity   and   of   Bethlehem   There were   -of the-   people

al   mondo,   felice   per   un   cavalluccio   di   legno
at the   world   happy   for   a   nice horse   of   wood
(in the)   {-uccio; affectionate}

scoperto   in   una   scarpa,   e   delle   barbe   grigie,   che
discovered   in   a   shoe   and   of the   beards   gray   that

piangevano   di   gioja   per   due   righe   di   rampini,
cried   of   joy   for   two   lines   of   nonsense

scarabocchiati e dedicati al nonno. Perchè
scribbled and dedicated to the grandfather Because

la felicità è per sè stessa una cosa leggera e
the happiness is by itself self a thing light and

porta in alto il cuore che sa contenerla.
carries in high the heart that knows how to contain it

--Gina! --gridò la voce della vecchia dal
Gina shouted the voice from the old lady from the

fondo della scala.
bottom of the stairs

Gina era fuggita. Scivolò al bujo dalle scale,
Gina was fled (She) slipped at the dark of the stairs
(had)

corse pel vicoletto, scappò via, mentre
ran down the alleyway escaped away while

accendevano i primi lampioni.
(they) lit the first (street) lamps

Non nevicava, ma tanta era stata la neve caduta
Not (it) snowed but so much was been the snow fallen
(had)

sui tetti, sui campanili, sugli abbaini, che
on the roofs on the bell towers on the dormer windows that

la città pareva lì per perdere il respiro.
the city seemed there for to lose the breath

Per la lunghezza delle vie, e per le
Because of the length of the streets and because of the

piazze profonde, le flammelle del gas, fatte
squares deep the flames of the gas made

rossigne, si stringevano in sè, come se
reddish themselves clung in themselves like if

temessero pure di dover morire di freddo; poche,
(they) feared also of to have to die of cold few

frettolose, le persone rasente ai muri;
hurried themselves the persons close to the walls

dagli archi delle botteghe chiuse, dalle finestre
from the arches of the shops closed of the windows

delle osterie, dalle case, traspariva quella luce
of the taverns of the houses shone through those lights

velata e calda, che ha dentro di sè il fumo
veiled and warm that (it) has inside of itself the smoke

delle pentole e la ciarla della gente allegra.
of the pots and the chatter of the people happy

Voltò per via Larga; di là pel corso,
(She) turned by street Larga from there by the Corso
      (via)

verso porta Romana, dov'era la strada per la
towards (the) Porta Romana where was the road for the
      (to)

Ghiacciata. Sperava di arrivarvi in meno
Ghiacciata (She) hoped -of- to arrive there in less

d'un'ora, non in carrozza, come sei mesi fa,
of an hour not in carriage like six months ago
(than an hour)

quando era partita, non fra due filari di
when (she) was left not between two files of
    (she had)

pioppi verdi, ma con un santo orgoglio, che la
poplars green but with a saintly pride that her

sorreggeva, che le riempiva gli occhi di lumi: al
supported that her filled the eyes of lights at the

di là dei lampioni, oltre i gabellini, oltre la
of there of the lamps beyond the gabelles beyond the

cerchia delle mura, che la serravano come l'anello
circle of the walls that her closed like the ring

d'una ruvida catena, anche in mezzo alla neve,
of a rough chain even in (the) middle at the snow
(of the)

alla nebbia, ai fossati, alle pozzanghere oscure,
at the fog at the ditches at the puddles dark

rasente ai cimiteri, la Gina vedeva la libertà;
close to the cemeteries -the- Gina saw the freedom

fuggiva, come se dietro i suoi passi corressero
fled as if behind -the- her passes ran

proprio ad inseguirla, e, voltandosi, guardava con
(it) itself to follow her and turning watched with

spavento la mole confusa e nebbiosa della città.
fear the heap confused and fogginess of the city

Presso i bastioni si trovò quasi perduta in
Close to the ramparts herself (she) found almost lost in

un campo di neve. Le guardie, in un cantuccio
a field of snow The guards in a corner

del dazio, stavano scaldandosi intorno a
of the duty station stood warming themselves around -to-

un braciere, discorrendo sottovoce con aria di
a brazier talking with a low voice with (an) air of

malcontento: al di là, quando cioè la Gina
discontent at the of there when that is -the- Gina

ebbe varcate anche le case del sobborgo, si
had passed also the houses of the suburb herself

trovò nel deserto addirittura, come le venne
(she) found in the desert even as her came

in mente d'aver letto, all'incirca, d'Elisabetta negli
in mind of to have read at the about of Elisabeth in the
(to)

"Esiliati in Siberia", quando giunge alle rive
Exiles in Siberia when (she) reaches -to- the shores

del Kama. La strada correva fra due fossati:
of the Kama The street ran between two ditches

non un carro, non un lume, non l'abbajare d'un
not a cart not a light not the barking of a

cane. Ma non per questo cessava d'andare; il
dog But not for this (she) stopped of to go the

negro, che sia sfuggito al flagello del piantatore,
black that has escaped the scourge of the planter

non respira con tanta voluttà l'aria delle selve,
not breathes with so much pleasure the air of the forest

quanto una coscienza, che si snodi da
as a conscience that itself unties from

un'abbiezione morale e torva, cerchi di tornare
an adversity moral and grim searches of to turn

alla stima di sè stessa. La Gina camminava nella
to the esteem of one self The Gina walked in the

neve, scendeva nelle pozze, nel ghiaccio, nella
snow descended in the pools in the ice in the

mota, contenta di dover vincere quegli ostacoli,
mud happy of to have to overcome those obstacles

come se, passando attraverso quella grande
as / if / passing / through / that / great

tribolazione, dovesse poi uscirne purificata.
tribulation / (she) must / then / come out of it / purified

Era scomparsa un giorno d'estate fra un
Was (She had) / disappeared / one / day / of summer / between / a

polverìo bianco: voleva ricomparire al
dust / white / (she) wanted / to reappear / at the

disotto d'un nembo di neve; così della Gina
underneath / -of- a / dark cloud / of / snow / like that / of the / Gina

si sarebbe dimenticato quel tempo, come se
itself / would have / forgotten / that / time / as / if

fosse stato un sogno.
was (it had) / been / a / dream

Camminò forse un'ora, senza mai sentire il
(She) walked / maybe / an hour / without / ever / to feel / the

freddo che le sbatteva sul viso; per la
cold / that / her / struck / on the / face / because of / the

lunga eccitazione del suo spirito, ella finiva,
long excitement of -the- her spirit she finished
(great)

sto per dire, col camminare sopra i propri
(I) stand for to say with the to walk on the own
(her)

pensieri. Certamente non vedeva l'ombra delle
thoughts Certainly not (she) saw the shadow of the

piante, nè i mucchi di ghiaja che costeggiano la
plants nor the piles of gravel that lined the

strada, sotto uno strato di neve; se li avesse
road under a layer of snow if them (she) had

veduti, ne avrebbe preso maggior spavento,
seen of it (she) would have taken major fright

quasi fossero tanti cataletti posti in fila. Molte
almost (there) were so many coffins set in file Many

sue amiche eran camminate al camposanto
her friends were walked to the cemetery
(had)

collo strato bianco, e dietro aveva cantato
with the layer (of) white and behind (she) had sung

anch'essa le litanie della Madonna, intonando il
also that one the litanies of the Madonna intoning the
(she also)

"Mater purissima". E cammina, e cammina. Ecco
Mother most pure And (she) walked and (she) walked See

finalmente che da' casolari, che sorgevano a
finally that from the homesteads that surged at
(stood)

destra e a manca della strada, sprofondati nel
right and at left of the road plunged in the

più fitto della notte, vede uscire, anche qui,
most thick of the night saw come out even here

quella luce velata e calda, che ha dentro di sè
that light veiled and hot that has inside of itself

il fumo delle pentole e la ciarla della gente
the smoke of the pots and the chatter of the people

allegra. Anche per questi luoghi morti e quasi
happy Also for these places dead and almost

disabitati era passato il santo Natale, caro ai
uninhabited was passed the holy Christmas dear to the
(had)

bambini, a suon di piva, circondato il capo
children at sound of bagpipe surrounded the head
(crowned)

d'edera e di muschio. Udiva delle canzoni,
of ivy and of moss (She) heard -of the- songs

ma la strada continuava sempre deserta, sempre
but the road continued always deserted always

bianca lungo i fossati in cui gorgogliava
white along the ditches in which gurgled

un'acqua cieca piena di misteri. Finchè le
a water blind full of mysteries Until that her

parve di ravvisare, allo svolto di una gran
(she) seemed of to recognize at the turn of a large

siepe secca, il luogo, dove sei mesi fa era
hedge dry the place where six months ago (she) was
(bare)

salita per la prima volta in carrozza, a guisa di
went out for the first time in carriage at guise of

certe povere ragazze delle favole, amate da
certain poor girls of the fairy tales loved by

principi. Quindi ravvisò anche il campanile
princes Then (she) saw back also the bell tower

aguzzo colla crocetta in cima, e fu per cadere
pointed with the cross in top and was for to fall

come morta; ma la tenne ritta il pensiero che
like dead but her kept straight the thought that

il più difficile era fatto e che, se Dio le avesse
the most difficult was done and that if God her had

dato di poter rientrare nella sua casa, non
given of to be able to re-enter in -the- her house not

solo ella avrebbe saputo trangugiare tutti i
only she would have known swallow all the

bocconi amari, ma si sarebbe chiamata felice
morsels bitter but herself would have called happy

di ottenere una scodella per carità e di far
of to obtain a bowl for charity and of to make

la serva alla sua matrigna. Giunta all'orlo
the servant to -the- her stepmother Arrived at the edge

della siepe di sambuco, che cingeva il giardino
of the hedge of elderberry that surrounded the garden

della Ghiacciata, guardò attraverso e vide che le
of the Ghiacciata looked through (it) and saw that the

finestre della vasta cucina brillavano; sotto stava
windows of the great kitchen shone under stood

il Toppa, attaccato all'organetto, e suonava una
the Toppa attached to the little organ and sounded a

bella mazurca; la sua faccia giallognola e
pretty mazurca -the- his face yellowish and

cretina sorrideva, mentre di dentro andavano e
stupid smiled while of inside went and

venivano delle ombre sulla cadenza della musica.
came of the shadows on the cadence of the music

La matrigna aveva invitato quel giorno Anselmo il
The stepmother had invited that day Anselmo the

mugnaio con suo figlio Gerola, un buon cristiano,
miller with his son Gerola a good Christian

zotico come un tronco, ma danaroso: da un
zealous   as   a   trunk   but   wealthy   from   a

pezzo la donna vi aveva messo gli occhi sopra
while   the   woman   there   had   put   the   eyes   on

per darlo, se si poteva, alla sua Carolina,
for   to give it   if   herself   (she) could   to -the-   her   Carolina

che un migliore non ne avrebbe potuto trovare
that   a   better   not   of it   would have   been able   to find

in questo mondo. Era stata contenta in cuor
in   this   world   (She) was   been   happy   in   heart
                              (She had)

suo che la Gina, sdrucciolando come aveva
hers   that   -the-   Gina   slipping   as   (she) had
        (when)

fatto, avesse sbarazzata la casa da una terribile
done   had   rid   the   house   of   a   terrible

rivale.
rival

La Gina si accostò all'uscio; non piangeva,
The   Gina   herself   approached   to the door   not   (she) cried

anzi, se si deve dirlo, si sentiva un coraggio
even if itself must to say it herself (she) felt a courage

e un'energia, di cui ella stessa si
and an energy of which she self herself

meravigliava. Il suo babbo era sempre il suo
amazed -The- her dad was always -the- her

babbo e una donna, messa alle strette, non ha
dad and a woman set to the squeeze not has

mai il cuore di respingere un'altra donna
ever the heart of reject an other woman

--pensava-- quando implora compassione per
(she) thought when (she) implores compassion for

amor di Dio.
love of God

Picchiò una volta e non fu udita.
(She) knocked one time and not was heard

Aspettò che il Toppa finisse di strimpellare e
(She) waited that the Toppa finished of to strum and
(until)

tornò   a picchiare più forte.
turned to   knock   more strong
(repeated)   (loud)

Questa volta qualcuno intese; la chiave scricchiolò
This   time   someone   noticed the key   creaked

e   il   volto della matrigna apparve nella fessura
and the face of the stepmother appeared in the crack

dell'uscio.
of the door

--Chi   è   a quest'ora?
Who   is (it) at   this hour

--Sono io,   la   Gina.
(It) is   I   -the-   Gina

Il   Toppa tornò   a suonare, e   il baccano, che
The Toppa turned to   play   and the noise   that
            (repeated)

sorse di dentro, impedì che altri potesse udire
rose from within prevented that others could hear

questo discorso.
this   discourse

--Sei tu, sgualdrinella? va via, non ti conosciamo.
Is (it) you   slut   go away not you   (we) know

--Per amor di Dio....
For   love of God

--Sei venuta in carrozza?
Are (you) come in   carriage

--Per carità, almeno per questa notte....
For charity at least for   this   night

--Questa notte meno che un'altra.
This   night less that an other
                      (than)

--E dove andare a quest'ora?
And where to go at this hour

--Va dalla tua mamma.
Go of the your mamma
    (to)

E   chiuse   l'uscio   con furore,   e   girò   due
And (she) closed the door with   fury   and turned two

volte la chiave: parve   a   un tratto che di
times the key   (it) seemed at a stretch that -of-

dentro si raddoppiasse la festa: la Carolina
inside itself doubled the party the Carolina

ballava con Gerola, e l'ostessa menava a tondo
danced with Gerola and the hostess led at circle

Anselmo il mugnaio, che non poteva reggersi
Anselmo the miller that not could support himself
(who)

sulle gambe. Il babbo dormiva nell'angolo nero
on the legs The dad slept in the corner black

del camino. La Gina non si accorse che
of the fireplace The Gina not herself noticed that

intanto ripigliava a nevicare; non si
meanwhile (it) picked up again to snow not herself

accorse nemmeno che l'acqua entrava nelle sue
(she) noticed not even that the water entered in -the- her

scarpe; nè che le vesti strisciavano per terra.
shoes nor that the dresses dragged on -the- ground

Non si sgomentò.
Not herself dismayed

--Andrò dalla mia mamma, --disse sottovoce, con
(I) will go of to my mamma (she) said softly with
(to) {under-voice}

un senso amoroso, la povera Gina. Conosceva
a sense (of) love the poor Gina (She) knew

bene la strada, perchè tutti gli anni soleva la
well the road because all the years (she) used the

mattina di Natale portarle un mazzo di fiori
morning of Christmas to carry her a mass of flowers

secchi, o un nastro ricamato. Quest'anno l'ora
dried or a ribbon embroidered This year the hour

era un po' tarda, ma la sua mamma l'avrebbe
was a bit late but -the- her mamma her would have

ricevuta.
received

Attraversò le vie deserte del paese: conobbe
(She) crossed the streets deserted of the village (she) knew

la strada del camposanto; spinse il cancello,
the road of the cemetery (she) pushed the gate
(to the) {field-holy}

che cedette.
that   yielded

--Essa m'ha aperto, --mormorò   la   Gina.
That one me has opened   murmured   -the- Gina

Traversò   il   piccolo campo, finchè   vide   una
(She) crossed the   small   field   until that (she) saw   a

croce di legno, mezz'arrovesciata nella neve; ne
cross   of wood   half toppled   in the snow of it

 sbarazzò le braccia, e cadde giù, esclamando
(she) cleared the   arms   and fell down   exclaiming

con uno   schianto: --M'han detto di venire da
with   a   break(ing voice) Me (they) have said   of to come by

te, mamma.
you   mamma

E   piangendo cercò di chiederle perdono;   si
And   crying searched of to ask her   pardon   herself

attaccò   al   legno con una stretta affettuosa di
attached   at the wood with   a   grasp affectionate   of

chi sente un cuore vicino, che risponde al suo.
who feels a heart close that responds to the hers

Poi chiuse gli occhi, per dormire accanto. La
Then (she) closed the eyes for to sleep next to (her) The

neve cadde alta tre spanne quella notte e tutti
snow fell high three spans that night and all

dicevano che avrebbe fatto bene alla
said that (it) would have done well to the

campagna.
countryside

Scaramucce
Skirmishes

SCARAMUCCE
Skirmishes

Anche la nostra divisione, già da venti giorni
Also -the- our division already from twenty days
(since)

accampata ad Oleggio, ricevette l'ordine di
camped at Oleggio received the orders -of-

raggiungere il grosso dell'esercito, che moveva
to reach the bulk of the army that moved

dal campo di Somma, per versarsi insieme
from the battlefield of Somma for to turn itself together

sulla divisione del generale Incaglia, incaricato di
on the division of the general Incaglia in charge of

difendere il Ticino. Noi eravamo i Bianchi,
to defend -the- Ticino We were the Whites

cioè colla fodera sul berretto, e il corpo
that is / with the / lining / on the / beret / and / the / corpse

dei Neri doveva rappresentare un esercito
of the / Blacks / had to / represent / an / army

nemico di sessanta mila uomini, pronto a
(of the) enemy / of / sixty / thousand / men / ready / to

ritirarsi sopra Varese; a noi era comandato di
retreat / above / Varese / and / us / was / commanded / -of-

vincere, e di coprirci di gloria, sparando
to win / and / -of- / to cover ourselves / of / glory / firing
(with)

coi fucili vuoti, fortuna che non capita
with -the- / rifles / empty / luck / that / not / happens

sempre nemmeno nelle battaglie da burla, sebbene
always / not even / in the / battles / of / joke / although
mock battles

nel mondo si veggano molti menare
in the / world / themselves / see / many / to beget

scalpore anche per più poco. Nessuna meraviglia
excitement / also / for / more little / No / wonder
for less

dunque, se alla vigilia stessa della manovra, molti
then if at the eve same of that maneuver many

cuori battessero come innanzi a una vera
hearts beat as before -to- a real

battaglia: ma il cuore batte spesso per nulla.
battle but the heart beats often for nothing

Alle tre di mattina il campo era già
At -the- three of (the) morning the battlefield was already

tutto in movimento. Splendevano ancora le stelle
all in movement Shone still the stars
The stars still shone

e la più bella luna che sia uscita dalle mani
and the most beautiful moon that was exited of the hands
had come out

del Creatore. La tromba dava i segnali, e
of the Creator The trumpet gave the signals and

dopo un gran frugare al bujo per terra, ci
after a large rummage at the dark by ground there
(on the)

avviammo in silenzio, carichi di sonno, per le
(we) walked in silence laden of sleep by the
(with)

strade biancheggianti e per le nere sodaglie alla
streets   whitewashed   and by the black garments at the
                              (with)

volta di Arona. Giunti   ai   brulli poggi di Cagnago
turn   of   Arona   Arrived at the barren hills   of   Cagnago

e   di Cumignago,   il   Monte Rosa cominciò   a
and   of   Cumignago   the   Monte   Rosa   began   to

disegnarsi e a colorirsi innanzi all'alba; ed ecco
draw itself   and to color itself   before   at the dawn and   see

a un tratto escono le prime fucilate dalle   siepi
at one stretch came out the   first   shots   from the hedges
   suddenly

e   dai   boschetti che coronano le alture; e
and from the   thickets   that   crowned   the heights and

noi avanti, rispondendo noi pure   colle   fucilate.
we   ahead   responding   us   also   with the   gunshots

I   Neri fuggivano come una nidiata di sorci,
The Blacks   fled   like   a   brood   of   mice

si   appiattavano dietro i cigli, sparavano
themselves   flattened   behind the gutters   fired

ancora quattro colpi, mostrando appena la fila
still four shots showing hardly the row

dei berretti, poi un'altra corserella; si
of the caps then an other little run themselves

vedevano comparire e sprofondarsi nelle
saw appear and subside themselves in the

vallette, e poi sempre avanti come se
little valleys and then always forward as if

giocassimo a rimpiattarelli.
(we) played at hide and seek

Così di poggio in poggio, di valloncello in
Like this from hill in hill from little valley in
(to) (to)

valloncello, ora diritti dietro un muro, ora sdraiati
little valley now standing behind a wall now lying
(then)

nei fossatelli, o terra terra, scaglionati nelle
in the ditches or earth earth spaced out in the
on the ground

piccole creste per una linea di forse sei miglia
small ridges for a line of maybe six mile
(in)

sulla destra del Ticino; finchè, occupate oramai
on the right of the Ticino until occupied by then

tutte le alture colla nostra artiglieria,
all the heights with -the- our artillery

si cominciò a discendere, a incalzare il
onself began to descend to press the
we began

nemico contro il fiume. Il giorno
enemy against the river The day

s'era fatto chiaro del tutto: il cielo non aveva
itself was made clear of the all the sky not had
become all clear

una ruga, e l'aria fresca della mattina ci lavava
a wrinkle and the air fresh of the morning you washed

il viso dell'ultima nebbia di sonno. Già ne
the face of the last fog of sleep Already from here

si apriva davanti il magnifico spettacolo del
itself opened in front the magnificent spectacle of the

Lago Maggiore, azzurro come il cielo, nella sua
Lake Major blue like the sky in -the- its

bella conca di montagne verdi, dipinte in cima
beautiful basin of mountains green painted in top

dal sole d'un bel colore di carminio.
of the sun of a beautiful color of carmine
(by the) (with a)

Nessuno di noi pensava più che si fosse a
Not one of us thought (any)more that oneself was at

una manovra. Il sangue, che trasalisce ai
a (army) maneuver The blood that jumps at the

primi colpi e che si riscalda alle prime
first blows and that itself warms up at the first

occhiate di sole, gli squilli di tromba, la voce
glances of the sun the squeals of trumpet the voices
(sounds)

dei capitani, il vedere correre e saltare i
of the captains the to see run and jump the

cannoni sopra i prati e piantarsi a urlare, le
cannons over the meadows and plant itself to roar the

vedette che passano via come freccie, il
lookouts that pass away like arrows the

luccichìo di qualche squadrone di cavalleria, che
gleam of some squadron of cavalry that

brilla in un nembo di polvere, superbo e
shines in a cloud of dust superb and

maestoso come una legione di arcangeli; tutto ciò
majestic like a legion of archangels all this

e più di tutto i vent'anni, che non pesano
and more of all the twenty years that not weigh

ancora sul sacco, fanno rincrescere quasi che
still on the sack make regret almost that
(bag)

non si faccia per davvero e che gli altri non
not oneself makes for real and that the others not

siano disposti a lasciarsi ammazzare. Due
are disposed to let themselves be killed Two

compagnie di Bianchi e di Neri, che si
companies of Whites and of Blacks that themselves

scontrarono l'anno scorso sulla piazzetta di
encounter the year past on the little square of

Divignano, mi dicono che, se non c'erano i
Divignano me told that if not there were the

superiori a fermarli, que' buoni figliuoli si
superiors to stop them those good boys each other

tagliavano a pezzi. E veramente l'illusione è sì
cut to pieces And truly the illusion is so

viva in questi istanti, che la ragione a stento può
alive in these instants that the reason at narrow can
        narrowly

trattenere la selvaggia natura, e vi passano
hold back the wild nature and there pass

per la fantasia idee stravaganti, che son
through the imagination ideas extravagant that are
        extravagant ideas

sorelle delle idee eroiche, e si capisce che
sisters of the ideas heroic and one understands what

cos'è lotta, che cos'è lo sterminio: non v'è
thing is struggle what thing is the extermination not there is

ragazzo di vent'anni, che, trovandosi a cavallo
(a) boy of twenty years that finding himself on (a) horse

fra — between
quattro — four
cannoni, — cannons
non — not
pensi — thinks
di — of
tagliare — to cut
il — the

mondo — world
con — with
un — one
colpo — stroke
di — of
spada. — (his) sword
Il — The
corpo — body
vi — you

par — seems
diventato — become
di — of
bronzo — bronze
sotto — under
la — the
giubba — tunic
di — of

panno. — cloth
Insomma, — In sum
non — not
state — stand
a — to
ridirlo, — laugh (at) it
ma — but
la — the

guerra — war
dev'essere — must be
una — a
bella — beautiful
cosa, — thing
forse — perhaps
ancora — even

più — more
bella — beautiful
dell'amore. — of the love
(than love)

Verso — Towards
le — the
nove — nine (o' clock)
giungemmo — (we) arrived
in — in
vista — sight
di — of
Arona. — Arona

In — In
questi — these
dintorni — surroundings
ha — has
(there is)
una — a
villetta — cottage
mio — of my
zio — uncle

Michele, — Michele
un — a
buon — good
uomo — man
che — that
ha — has
fatto — made
molti — much
denari — money

col sapone e colle candele steariche, non
with the | soap | and | with the | candles stearic | not
stearic candles

sapendo nulla dei grandi problemi che
knowing | nothing | of the | great | problems | that

travagliano la pellegrina umanità. Sarei stato
torment | the | pilgriming | humanity | (I would be) (I would have) | been

ben felice, se il caso mi avesse portato a dare
well (quite) | happy | if | the | case (chance) | me | had | led | to | give

una capatina alla villa Teresa (Teresa era il nome
a | visit | to the | villa | Teresa | Teresa | was | the | name

della mia povera zia), non perchè in casa di
of -the- | my | poor | aunt | not | because | in | (the) house | of

mio zio Michele la tavola sia quasi sempre
my | uncle | Michele | the | table | is | almost | always

preparata, ma per la gloria di comparire agli
prepared (laden with food) | but | for | the | glory | of | to appear | at the

occhi di mia cugina, bello di polvere,
eyes | of | my | cousin | beautiful | of (with) | dust

abbronzato   dal   sole,   cioè,   come   dicono   i
bronzed   by the   sun   that is   as   say   the

romanzieri,   irresistibile.   Mio   zio,   uomo   di   vecchia
novelists   irresistible   My   uncle   man   of   old (long)

esperienza,   non   aveva   mai   veduto   di   buon   occhio
experience   not   had   ever   seen   of   good   eye

gli   avvocati,   e   quando   seppe   ch'io   m'ero   dato
the   lawyers   and   when   (he) knew   that I   myself was   given

allo   studio   della   legge,   crollò   la   testa,   come   se
to the   study   of the   law   collapsed   the   head   like   if

si   trattasse   d'un   ladro   mestiere.   Forse   il   suo
itself   dealt   of a   thief   profession   Maybe   -the-   his

ideale   (voglio   dire   il   genero   de'   suoi   sogni)   non
ideal   (I) want   to say   the   son-in-law   of   his   dreams   not

era   un   pitocchello   di   qualche   ingegno,   ricco
was   a   pith   of   some   genius   rich

soltanto   di   belle   speranze,   ma   qualche   cosa   di
only   of   beautiful   expectations   but   some   thing   of
(great)

più sostanzioso, di più palpabile. Perciò non
more substance of more tangible Therefore not

posso dire nemmeno che mio zio mi amasse
(I) could say even that my uncle me loved

come la pupilla degli occhi suoi; tuttavia la
like the pupil of -the- eyes his nevertheless -the-
the apple of his eyes

mia bionda cuginetta Elisa, un diavoletto che
my blond little cousin Elisa a little devil that

avrebbe colle sue moine disarmata la Prussia,
would have with the her flattery disarmed -the- Prussia

spadroneggiava nel cuore del babbo, e se per
disgraced in the heart of the dad and if for

un capriccio avesse voluto sposare uno
a whim (she) had wanted to marry a

spazzacamino, il babbo avrebbe benedetto anche
chimney sweep the dad would have blessed also

lo spazzacamino.
the chimney sweep

Io mi lusingavo d'essere qualche cosa di più: e
I myself flattered of to be some thing of more and

sebbene, prima che mi cingessi un brando,
although before that myself girded a sword
{poetic}

potessi anche sembrare un mattarello di poco
(I) could even seem a rolling pin of little
(loggerhead)

giudizio e considerare la Lisa come una
judgement and consider -the- Lisa like a

ragazzina, oggi ero un volontario e caporale. Il
young girl today (I) was a volunteer and corporal The

soldato aveva aggiustato l'uomo, e dopo quasi un
soldier had adjusted the man and after almost a
(mended)

mese di vita selvaggia, all'erba, sotto la tenda
month of life wild at the grass under the tent

all'aria, al sole, la figura snella di mia cugina
at the air at the sun the figure slim of my cousin

mi tornava davanti come una dolce visione,
me returned in front like a sweet vision

mentre, appoggiato al mio fucile, procuravo di
while leaning at the my rifle (I) tried of

discernere qualche cosa di bianco a una finestra
to discern some thing of white at a window

della villa.
of the villa

Intanto che tutt'assorto nella contemplazione di
While that all absorbed in the contemplation of

due gelosie verdi, carezzavo una dolce
two (window) shutters green (I) caressed a sweet

speranza col pensiero, il capitano, forse
hope with the thought the captain maybe

ispirato da Dio, ordina al mio tenente di
inspired by God ordered to -the- my lieutenant -of-

prendere con sè quattro o cinque uomini e
to take with himself four or five men and

di occupare proprio la villetta dalle gelosie
-of- to occupy precisely the little villa of the shutters
(with the)

verdi, che per trovarsi in una spianata elevata
green that for to find itself in a area elevated

sul declivio, dominava dal suo terrazzo una
on the slope dominated from the its terrace a

buona parte del fiume. Il tenente mi dice:
good part of the river The lieutenant me says

--Venga anche lei, caporale.
Come also you corporal

Non aveva ancora terminate queste parole, che io
Not (he) had yet finished these words that I

camminavo già sul viottolo che conduce alla
walked already on the path that led to the

palazzina, fra due siepi di bosco, lieto e
little palace between two hedges of wood happy and
{-ina; diminutive}

trionfante. --Questa volta, caro zio, --dicevo
triumphant This time dear uncle (I) said

fra me, --conquistiamo la posizione: l'avvocato
between me (we) conquer the position the lawyer
by myself

ritorna a capo d'un esercito, nè basta una
returns at (the) head of an army nor is enough a

muraglia di sapone a questi assalti.
miserable wall of soap to these assaults
{-aglia; pejorative}

Strada facendo, il mio signor tenente, un
Road making -the- my lord lieutenant a
Along the way

vanerello ancor fresco d'accademia, con un
little vain one still fresh from (the) academy with a
(light weight)

finestrino di vetro nella cassa dell'occhio sinistro,
little window of glass in the case of the eye left

non cessava dal far paragoni fra il
not ceased of the to make comparisons between the

Verbano e il Lago di Garda, dove i suoi
Verbano and the Lago di Garda where the his

avevano una villa: suo padre era marchese, e il
had a villa his father was Marquis and the

tenentino non disperava di diventare un giorno
little lieutenant not despair of to become one day

almeno generale, e tante altre cose andava
at least general and many other things (he) went

dicendomi, per dimostrarmi ch'egli era ricco,
telling me for to show me that he was rich

marchese, bravo cavalcatore, e amato da tutte le
Marquis good rider and loved by all the

donne. Ma per conto mio pensavo alla
women But for count (of) mine (I) thought at the

meraviglia di mio zio e della mia cuginetta,
surprise of my uncle and of -the- my little cousin

quando mi avessero conosciuto; pensavo che,
when me (they) had known (I) thought that
they would meet me

finiti gli studi dell'Università, sarei stato
finished the studies of the University (I) would be been
(I would have)

dottore e che la fortuna di questo mondo
doctor (in law) and that the fortune of this world

non la si fa solamente col sapone e
not it itself makes only with the soap and

colle candele steariche; pensavo che avrei
with the candles Stearic (I) thought that (I) would have

saputo rendere felice la mia bella cugina,
known to render happy -the- my beautiful cousin
     (to make)

anche a costo delle sue duecentomila lire di
also at cost of -the- her two hundred thousand lire of

dote.
dowry

Intanto giungemmo al cancello del giardino.
Meanwhile (we) arrived at the gate of the garden

Al rivedere que' viali, quelle piante, que'
At the to see again those avenues those plants those
   At seeing again

luoghi pieni d'ombra e di frescura, que' sedili,
places full of shade and of coolness those seats

quelle statue coperte di muschio, che mi
those statues covered of moss that me
                 (with)

ricordavano una lunga storia di giuochi, di capricci,
reminded a long history of games of caprices

di lagrime e di versi sbagliati, mi pareva di
of tears and of songs incorrect me (it) seemed of

diventar piccino, e il cuore batteva anche a
to become small (again) and the heart beat also to

me come alla vigilia d'una vera battaglia.
me like at the eve of a real battle

Tip, il grosso Tip, fu il primo che ci corse
Tip the big Tip was the first that us ran
{the dog}

incontro abbajando. Allora il sor tenente,
towards barking Then the Mr lieutenant

accostandosi l'occhialino, --Caporale, --disse, --lei
touching himself the lorgnette Corporal (he) said you

si fermi accanto a questo pino con due
yourself stop next to this pine with two

uomini e non perda di vista il campanile di
men and not loose of sight the bell tower of
loose sight of

Golasecca.
Golasecca

Condusse   e   piantò gli altri uomini in diversi
(He) led   and planted the other men   in diverse

punti, poi   si   avviò solo   verso   la   villetta,   che
points then   himself set off alone towards the little villa that

distava   dal   mio pino un quaranta passi, per
was away from -the-   my   pine a   fourty   steps   for

rendere omaggio   ai   padroni di   casa.   Elisa gli
to render homage to the   patrons of (the) house Elisa him

venne incontro per la prima.
came   to meet   for the first
                 (as)

Vestiva, come   di solito, un po' capricciosamente;
Dressed   like   of usual   a   bit capriciously
                 (as)

i   capelli biondi, sciolti, scendevano   sopra   un
the hairs   blonds   loose   came down   over   a
     hair blond

vestito quasi bianco, allacciato   ai   ginocchi da
dress   almost white   fastened   to the   knees   by

una fascia rossa di fuoco. Da   sei   mesi   o forse
a   band   red   of fire   Since six   months or maybe

più che io non la rivedevo, la ragazzina s'era
more that I not her saw again the little girl herself was

fatta alta e complessa, e la moda aiutava a
made tall and intricate and the fashion helped to

stringerla in vita e a darle attraenti
tighten her in life and to give her attractions
tighten her up

disuguaglianze.
without equal

Il sor tenente, un gatto vecchio che sapeva
The Mr lieutenant a cat old that knew

arrampicarsi, portò la mano alla visiera, si
to climb himself carried the hand to the visor himself

piegò come si piega un bastoncino di giunco,
bent like itself bends a stick of reed

sussurrò delle paroline sorridenti, Dio sa quali
whispered -of the- little words smiling God knows which

sciocchezze! Elisa arrossì un poco, sorrise
nonsense Elisa blushed a little smiled

anch'essa e corse ad avvisare il babbo.
also she   and   ran   to   warn   the   father

Io intanto non perdevo di vista il campanile di
I   meanwhile not   lost   of sight the bell tower   of
                       lost sight of

Golasecca.
Golasecca

Elisa aprì le persiane della terrazza, e dopo un
Elisa opened the   shutters   of the   terrace   and after   an

istante uscì anche lo zio Michele, sotto un
instant came out also   the uncle   Michele   under   a

gran cappello di paglia. Il buon uomo pareva
big   hat   of   straw   The good   man   seemed

beato che la villa Teresa diventasse un punto
blessed   that the villa   Teresa   became   a   point
(overjoyed)

strategico da far parlare i giornali, e portò
strategic   of to make   talk   the newspapers and carried

egli stesso sotto il padiglione della terrazza due
him   self   under   the   pavilion   of the   terrace   two

lunghi cannocchiali, coi quali pretendeva di
long telescopes with the which (he) claimed of

vedere le fabbriche di candele steariche anche
to see the factories of candles Stearic even

nel mondo della luna. Elisa, una discreta
in the world of the moon Elisa a discreet

chiaccherina quando voleva, avviò una grande
chatter when (she) wanted started a great

conversazione col tenente che col braccio
conversation with the lieutenant that with the arm

teso andava via via, segnandole i punti
outstretched walked away away pointing out to her the points

principali delle operazioni di campo,
main of the operations of (the) battlefield

intercalando, suppongo, delle scipitezze, perchè le
interspersing (I) suppose of the tasteless jokes because the

manovre son cose serie, e non si ride delle
maneuvers are things serious and not oneself laughs of the

cose serie.
things serious

Io intanto non perdevo di vista il campanile di
I meanwhile not lost of sight the bell tower of
                 lost sight of

Golasecca.
Golasecca

Vedendo che non c'era modo di attirare
Seeing that not there was manner of to attract

l'attenzione di Elisa un poco anche sul caporale,
the attention of Elisa a but also on the corporal

mi volto a' miei due soldati, li squadro
myself (I) turned to the my two soldiers them squared
                                          (eyed)

da cima a fondo, e scoperti due bottoni d'una
from top to bottom and discovered two buttons of one

uosa "che non c'erano": --Pare impossibile,
gaiter that not there were (It) seems impossible

--strillai schiamazzando come un'oca del
(I) shouted cackling like a goose from the

Campidoglio, --pare impossibile, sacr.... che si
Capitol (it) seems impossible holy... that oneself

portino di quelle porcherie; testa di gatto! perchè
carries of those swineries head of cat why
such filth

mancano que' due bottoni? E zitto, o vi butto
lack those two buttons And quiet or you (I) throw

in prigione per tre settimane, sacr.....
in prison for three weeks holy...

Ma la conversazione del sor tenente era così
But the conversation of the Mr lieutenant was so

piacevole che l'Elisa non s'accorse delle mie
pleasurable that -the- Elisa not -herself- noticed of -the- my

bestemmie. Mi pentivo di non aver detto
blasphemies -Myself- (I) regretted of not to have said

prima al tenente che mio zio era mio zio, e
first to the lieutenant that my uncle was my uncle and

mia cugina qualche cosa di più di una cugina: ma
my cousin some thing of more of a cousin but

non l'avevo fatto per antipatia, per ignoranza.
not it (I) had done for antipathy for ignorance

Peggio per me! Però mia cugina sapeva bene il
Worse for me But my cousin knew well the

numero del mio reggimento, e quel numero
number of -the- my regiment and that number

l'aveva sotto gli occhi; perchè non avrebbe dovuto
she had under the eyes why not would have must
                                              should have

domandare al tenente se conosceva il caporale
ask to the lieutenant if (he) knew the corporal

così e così? Il tenente presentò a mio zio,
such and so The lieutenant presented to my uncle

com'era giusto, anche il suo biglietto di visita,
like was right also -the- his ticket of visit
                                              business card

con tanto di corona sopra: mio zio fe' due
with so much of crown on (it) my uncle made two

occhi di barbagianni, s'inchinò, strinse le labbra
eyes of barn owl himself bowed tightened the lips

come se assaggiasse del vin santo, passò il
like if (he) tasted -of the- wine holy passed the

biglietto alla figlia, che si profuse anch'essa
ticket to the daughter that herself profused also she
(card)

in riverenze. Corbezzole! un marchesino non
in reverences Arbutus berries a little Marquis not
{expression of surprise}

capita tutti i giorni tra' piedi; non si
understands all the days between the feet not oneself

sa mai ciò che un marchesino può diventare.
knows ever that what a little Marquis can become

Mio zio avrebbe voluto essere una saponetta per
My uncle had wanted to be a little soap for

le sue belle mani, o una torcia stearica per
-the- his beautiful hands or a torch Stearic for
(candle)

fargli lume.
to make him light

Io intanto non perdevo di vista il campanile di
I meanwhile not lost of sight the bell tower of
lost sight of

Golasecca.
Golasecca

Il mio bonissimo zio, dopo avere stretta fra
-The- my very good uncle after to have held between

le sue la mano del marchesino, distese sopra
-the- his the hand of the little Marquis spread out over

un tavolino una carta geografica della provincia,
a little table a card geographic of the province

dove il tenente continuò la sua lezione, seduto
where the lieutenant continued -the- his lesson seated

accanto all'Elisa. Vi fu un momento che
besides to -the- Elisa There was a moment that

questa abbassò la testa per meglio orientarsi,
this one lowered the head for better to orient herself

e il tenente abbassò la sua, rasentando colle
and the lieutenant lowered -the- his grazing with the

labbra i capelli della mia cara cugina. La
lips the hairs of -the- my dear cousin The

battaglia era veramente disastrosa per me. Mentre
battle was truly disastrous for me While

pareva che i due eserciti volessero riposare un
(it) seemed that the two armies wanted to rest a

poco, le fucilate rincominciarono nel mio cuore:
bit the shots recommenced in -the- my heart
(firing)

e son fucilate che fanno squarci, non c'è
and (they) are shots that make gashes not there is

muro che tenga! Mio zio, facendosi visiera
(a) wall that stops (them) My uncle making himself (a) visor
(binoculars)

colle due mani, cercava il nemico in su quel
with the two hands searched the enemy in on that one

di Sesto Calente, e gridava: --Si restringono;
of Sixth Calente and shouted They are retracting
(are pulling back)

--mentre il tenente sussurrava delle paroline
while the lieutenant whispered -of the- little words
(sweet words)

topografiche all'orecchio di Elisa.
geographical at the ear of Elisa
(in the ear)

--Signor tenente! --gridai, saltando a un tratto
Mr. lieutenant (I) shouted jumping at a stretch
all of a sudden

sul terrazzino.
on the little terrace

La mia bella cugina si scosse, mi riconobbe
-The- my beautiful cousin herself shook me recognized

e gridò: --To', Pierino.
and shouted You Pierino

--Sei tu, nipote mio? --esclamò mio zio
Are you (that) nephew (of) mine exclaimed my uncle

con poco entusiasmo.
with little enthusiasm

--Cos'avete, caporale? --interruppe il tenente
What do (you) have corporal interrupted the lieutenant

in un modo insolito; e voltosi a mio zio:
in a manner rude and turning himself to my uncle

--Perdonerà, ma vi può essere un pericolo.
(You) will pardon but there can be a danger

--La patria, la patria anzi tutto,
The fatherland the fatherland (is) indeed everything

--osservò quel sant'uomo di mio zio Michele.
observed that saintly man of my uncle Michele

--Una compagnia di Neri passeggia sul
A company of Blacks passes on the
(black uniforms)

sagrato di Golasecca, --dissi affannosamente e,
churchyard of Golasecca (I) said breathless and

voltomi alla Lisa, le chiesi: --Come stai?
turning myself to -the- Lisa her (I) asked How are (you)

--Sto bene... --rispose confusamente.
(I) am well (she) answered confused

--È ben sicuro d'averli veduti! --tornò a
And well sure of to have them seen turned to
(continued)

dimandare il tenente un po' seccato.
ask the lieutenant a bit dried out
(annoyed)

--Co' miei occhi... --ripicchiai insolentemente.
With my eyes (I) repeated insolently

--Prenda   i   suoi uomini   e   faccia   un   giro per
Take   -the- your   men   and   make   a   turn   by

tutta   la   vigna,   osservando attentamente tutti   i
all   the vineyard   observing   attentively   all   the

punti all'intorno: anzi   sarà   bene   che   salga
points -at the- around indeed (it) will be   well   that (you) go up

su qualche pianta.
on   some   plant

Mentre   il   tenente parlava,   i   miei occhi erano
While   the lieutenant talked   -the- my   eyes   were

inchiodati addosso   all'Elisa   che abbassò i   suoi.
fixed   on   -to the- Elisa that lowered the hers

--Ha   capito,   caporale?
(Do you) have understood   corporal

--Sissignore, --risposi   a   denti stretti.
Yes-sir   (I) answered at/(with) teeth clenched

--E non perda di vista....
And not loose of   sight

--Ho capito! --gridai, interrompendolo, e
(I) have understood (I) shouted interrupting him and

voltai le spalle.
(I) turned the shoulders

--Se i Neri ci lasceranno un po' di pace, le
If the Blacks you let a bit of peace you

permetterò di far colazione con suo zio.
(I) will permit -of- to make breakfast with your uncle
(to have)

--Abbi pazienza, nipote mio: la patria anzi
Have patience nephew (of) mine the fatherland indeed

tutto. --E mio zio rideva.
all And my uncle laughed

La parola colazione il marchesino non l'aveva
The word breakfast the little marquis not it had

fatta sonare per nulla: mio zio, che non ci
made sound for nothing my uncle that not (of) it

pensava nemmeno, si risvegliò come di
thought not even himself rose as of

soprassalto;   pensò   che il povero marchese
(a) jump up   (he) thought   that the   poor   marquis
(a startle)

poteva aver fame, e mentre io facevo il giro
could   have hunger and while   I   made   the turn
       be hungry

della vigna, presto presto, un tovagliolo, un pajo
of the vineyard quick   quick   a   napkin   a   pair

d'uova fritte, una bistecca,   fra   una fucilata e
of egg   fried   a   steak   between   a   shot   and

l'altra, un bicchierino di bordò con un pezzettino
the other a   small glass   of bordeaux with   a   small piece

di ghiaccio. Questo dev'essere accaduto, mentre io
of   ice   This   must be   happened   while   I

andavo in cerca di una pianta... per impiccare
went   in search of   a   plant   for   to hang

l'amor mio,   le mie speranze, le mie illusioni.
the love (of) mine -the- my   hopes   -the- my   illusions

Infatti, quando tornai presso il pino della mia
In fact   when (I) returned by   the pine of -the- my

disperazione, in vista del campanile di Golasecca,
desperation — in — view — of the — bell tower — of — Golasecca

il tavolino era imbandito sotto il padiglione, al
the little table — was — set — under — the — pavilion — at the

fresco, e il tenente, servito dalle mani stesse di
fresh (air) — and — the — lieutenant — served — of the (by the) — hands — same — of

mia cugina, mangiava come un eroe di Omero.
my — cousin — ate — like — a — hero — of — Homer

Gli occhi a un tratto mi si offuscarono. Se
The — eyes — at one stretch (all of a sudden) — me — themselves — clouded up — If

invece di semplice polvere avessi avuto del
instead — of — simple — (gun) powder — (I) had — had — of the

piombo nel mio fucile, chi mi assicura che
lead — in -the- — my — rifle — that — me — assured — that

Pierino non avrebbe fatto uno sproposito?
Pierino — not — would have — made — a — proposal

Rimasi più d'un quarto d'ora in una specie
(I) remained — more (than a) — of a — quarter — of (an) hour — in — a — sort

d'estasi rabbiosa, il tempo cioè che il tenente
of ecstasy angry the time what is that the lieutenant

impiegò per trangugiare i due piatti freddi;
employed for to swallow the two dishes cold

quindi la compagnia entrò in sala, forse a
therefore the company entered in room maybe to

prendere un caffè. No, la guerra non è più
take a coffee No the war not is more

bella dell'amore!
beautiful of the love
(than love)

--Essa non ha un briciolo di cuore per me,
That one not has a shred of heart for me
(She)

--andavo dicendo, --è una civetta che sogna
(I) went saying (it) is a coquette that dreams

il marchesino e la carrozza! essa mi
(of) the little marquis and the carriage that one me

lascerebbe anche morire di fame, se io potessi
would leave also die of hunger if I could

ancora — still
aver — have
fame! — hunger
Povere — Poor
mie — my
speranze, — hopes
My poor hopes

poveri — poor
miei — my
sogni!-- — dreams
my poor dreams

A — At
queste — these
lamentazioni — laments
s'intrecciò — itself introduced
una — a
musica — music

malinconica — melancholy
che — that
uscì — exited
dalla — from the
villa. — villa
Era — (It) was
lei — her
che — that

faceva — made
sentire — hear
al — to the
tenente — lieutenant
la — the
"Prière — Prayer
à — to
la — the

Madone" — Madonna
sul — on the
piano-forte, — piano forte
una — a
musica — music
che — that

non — not
giungeva — arrived
nuova — new
al — to -the-
mio — my
cuore, — heart
che — that
mi — me
had arrived before

aveva — had
insegnate — taught
tante — so many
belle — beautiful
cose! — things
Erano — (They) were

lagrime — tears
vere, — real
che — that
ora — now
riempivano — filled
gli — the
occhi — eyes

(non state a dirlo) e che io asciugai colla
not stop to tell it and that I dried with the
I do not keep quiet about it

manica ruvida del mio cappotto. Quando alzai
sleeve rough of the my coat When (I) raised

il viso, vidi mio zio sul terrazzino, curvo,
the face (I) saw my uncle on the little terrace bent

colle mani appoggiate alle ginocchia, intento a
with the hands rested at the knees intent on

speculare nel cannocchiale le mosse dei Neri:
speculating in the telescope the movements of the Blacks
(viewing)

la musica era cessata e il buon uomo gridava:
the music was stopped and the good man shouted
(had)

--Si restringono sempre.--
Themselves (they) draw back always
(still)

Io allora, col mio fucile stretto fra le
I then with -the- my rifle clasped between the

mani, col passo leggiero d'uno scoiattolo,
hands with the step light of a squirrel

saltando — sulla — sabbia, — eccomi — sul — terrazzino,
jumping — on the — sand — see me (here I am) — on the — little terrace

anzi — fin — quasi — alla — persiana, — prima — che — mio — zio
indeed — end (up to) — almost — to the — shutter — before — that — my — uncle

se — ne — accorga; — mi — arresto, — arresto — i
himself — of it — realizes — myself — (I) stop — (I) stop — the

moti — del — cuore, — spingo — il — capo — verso
movements — of the — heart — push — the — head — towards

l'entrata — e — l'occhio — verso — il — piano-forte, — e,
the entrance (the opening) — and — the eye — towards — the — piano forte — and

non — vedendo — più — il — campanile — di — Golasecca,
not — seeing — (any) more — the — bell tower — of — Golasecca

sparo — in — aria — un — colpo, — io — non — so — perchè, — un
fire — in — (the) air — a — shot — I — not — know — why — a

colpo — che — rimbombò — come — un — temporale. — Mio — zio
shot — that — thunders — like — a — storm — My — uncle

Michele — saltò — a — cavallo — del — cannocchiale, — Elisa
Michele — jumps — at — horse on top — of the — telescope — Elisa

gettò un grido e svenne nelle braccia... d'una
utters a scream and faints in the arms of an

poltrona; i miei soldati sparsi nella vigna,
armchair and my soldiers scattered in the vineyard

credendo di far bene, risposero con una salva, e
believing of to do well answer with a salvo and

a questa risposero altre salve dei nostri, rimasti
at that answer other salvos of -the- ours remained

sulla strada, che temevano d'un'imboscata. Tutto
on the road that fear of an ambush All

il campo fu messo sottosopra e per poco non
the field was put upside down and for little not

ne andava di mezzo la fortuna della giornata.
of it went of half the fortune of the day

Io, appoggiato al muro, pallido, irrigidito,
I leaned against the wall pale stiff

non sapevo più in che mondo mi trovassi.
not knew (any) more in what world myself (I) found

Della lunga predica che il tenente infuriato e
Of the long serman that the lieutenant furious and

rosso in viso fece sonare al mio orecchio, io
red in (the) face made sound at the my ear I
(in)

non intesi se non che, giunti a Milano, egli mi
not understood if not that arrived at Milan he me

avrebbe condannato a un mese di prigione e a
would have condemned to one month of prison and to

tre di consegna in caserma.
three of consignment in barracks

E mantenne la parola da vero gentiluomo.
And (he) maintained the word of (a) real gentleman

Ne' panni suoi avrei fatto di più; ma
In the shoes (of) his (I) would have done of more but

quando mi fu concesso di uscire, tutto era
when me (it) was allowed of to get out all was

finito, la battaglia era perduta.
finished the battle was lost
(over)

Sei mesi dopo ricevetti un bigliettino malinconico
Six months after (I) received a note melancholy

di mio zio, che mi pregava di andare a
from my uncle that me begged of to go and
(who)

trovarlo e di perdonargli molte cose: non seppi
to find him and of to pardon him many things not (I) knew

resistere alla tentazione, e, sebbene avessi
to resist to the temptation and although (I) had

giurato di non porre più il piede nella sua
sworn of not to put (any) more the foot in the his

casa, vi andai, Non era più lo zio d'una
house there (I) went Not (he) was (any) more the uncle of one

volta. Mi fece sedere accanto, mi prese
time Me (he) made sit besides me grasped

malinconicamente la mano, mentre gli occhi gli
melancholic the hand while the eyes him

si riempivano di lagrime.
themselves filled of tears

--Elisa? --balbettai con voce tremante.
Elisa   (I) stammered   with   voice   trembling

--È   malata.--
(She) is   sick
       {euphemistic for pregnant}

Il   nemico era passato devastando il   paese.
The   enemy   was   passed   devastating   the countryside
                  (had)

Parlatene Alla Zia
Talk about it with the Aunt

PARLATENE ALLA ZIA
Talk of it   To the Aunt

NICOLÒ
Nicolo

(è   un giovinetto maturo, che ha   già   fatto le
(he) is a   youth   mature   that has already got   the
                mature young man

sue   campagne. Gran   buon   diavolo   nel   fondo.
his   campaigns   Big   good   devil   in the   bottom
       {army service}

Siamo in   campagna   nella villa d'Incirano. Nicolò
(We) are in (the) countryside in the   villa   of Incirano   Nicolo

in   cappello di paglia   e   in   abito grigio chiaro,
in   hat   of   straw   and in   dress   gray   clear
(with)   (light)

entra   dal   giardino e   dice a qualcuno che non
enters from the   garden   and says to someone   that not

si   vede:)
oneself   sees
is visible

--Grazie, aspetterò.
Thanks   (I) will wait

(Dà   un'occhiata intorno,   si   passa una mano
(He) gives   an eye   around   himself passes a   hand
         (a glance)

nei capelli e   con un breve sospiro d'affanno
in the hairs   and with a   short   sigh   of breath

dice:)
says

--Eccomi qua. Il cuore mi batte come se volesse
See myself here The heart me beats like if (it) wanted

scoppiare. Ho   paura di aver   già   fatto un
to burst   (I) have fear of to have already made a

passo falso. Basta! sono ancora in tempo a
step   wrong Enough (I) am   still   in   time to

pentirmi e se   sarà il caso,   infilerò
repent myself and if (it) will be the   case   (I) will go through

l'uscio.
the exit

(Si   abbandona su un divano.)
Himself   abandons   on   a   sofa
   He lets himself fall

--Sicuro, Nicolò: se non   concludi   qualche cosa
Certainly   Nicolo   if   not   (you) conclude   some   thing

quest'oggi, tu morirai   nel   tuo letto in odore di
  this day   you   will die   in -the- your   bed   in   smell   of
  (today)

verginità. No, no: è   tempo che tu   la   pigli
  virginity   No   no   (it) is   time   that   you   her   pick

questa moglie benedetta! Vedi?
  this   wife   blessed   (You) see

(va   a   guardarsi   in uno specchio.)
Goes   to   look at himself   in   a   mirror

--Tu sei arrivato a quell'età in cui, se il frutto
  You   are   arrived   at   that age   in   which   if   the   fruit
  (have)

non si coglie, casca   in   terra a marcire. Non
  not itself catches (it) fals   in   ground to   rot   Not
        is caught   (on the)

sei   un brutto mostro: che, che?
(you) are   an   ugly   monster   what   what

(carezzandosi i baffi.)
caressing himself the mustache

--Puoi passare ancora per un giovanotto in gambe,
(I) can   pass   still   for   a   young man   in   legs
                                                     sporty

ma.... qua e là comincia a spuntare qualche
but   here   and   there   start   to   emerge   some

capello meno nero degli altri. Certe mattine
hair   less   black   of the   others   Certain   mornings
                              (then the)

hai la ciera d'un uomo che ha dormito male
(you) have   the   look   of a   man   that   has   slept   bad
              {cera}

(parlando alla sua immagine.)
speaking   to -the- his   image
                        (reflection)

--Sicuro, signor Nicolò: quel vivere di qua, di
Certainly   Mr.   Nicolo   that   living   -of- here   -of-

là, sulle trattorie, sui caffè, sui "clubs", in
there   on the   taverns   on the   cafes   on the   clubs   in
      (in the)

compagnia di scapoloni pari suoi non è più
company of bachelors similar to yours not is more

una vita fatta per lei.... Lei digerisce male, lei
a life made for you You digest badly you

dorme male, diventa sempre più brontolone,
sleep badly (you) become always more grouchy

bisbetico, incontentabile e a lungo andare
cantankerous unsatisfied and at long go
in the long run

finirà col fare uno sproposito. Chi non
(you) will finish with the to make a mistake Who not

si marita a tempo, sposa la morte prima
himselfs marries at time marries the death before
(in)

del tempo; tranne il caso in cui si
of the time except the case in which oneself

sposa la serva
(one) marries the servant

(torna a sedere.)
(he) returns to sit

--Mia sorella Giacomina, che da un pezzo mi ha
My sister Giacomina that from a while me has

sul cuore, la settimana scorsa mi disse:
on the heart the week (that) ran me said
last week

--Nicolò, c'è una ragazza che va bene per te:
Nicolo there is a girl that goes well for you

anzi ce ne sono due: le sorelle Bellini, due
even there of them are two the sisters Bellini two

care creaturine sui ventitrè l'una, sui
dear little creatures on the twenty-three the one on the
(about) (about)

ventiquattro l'altra, non troppo giovani e
twenty-four the other not too young and

nemmeno troppo stagionate, un po' disgraziate
neither too seasoned a bit unfortunate
(aged)

nella famiglia, ma buone, belle, con qualche po'
in the family but good beautiful with some bit
(a little)

di sostanza. Tu non hai che a scegliere. Esse
of substance You not have that to choose They
(money) (than)

vivono a Incirano con una zia che fa loro da
live at Incirano with an aunt that makes them of (servers) (as)

madre, perchè le poverine hanno perduto i
mother because the poor ones have lost the

parenti e non hanno si può dire nessuno
parents and not have oneself can say no one (anyone)

al mondo. Sotto questo aspetto tu fai quasi
at the (in the) world Under this respect you do almost

un'opera di carità. Va a mio nome, cerca della zia,
a work of charity Go at my name find of the aunt

mettiti nelle sue mani e lascia fare alla
put yourself in the her hands and let make to the

provvidenza.
providence (fate)

--Eccomi qui. Ora le vedrò e dovrò
See me here Now them (I) will see and will have to

scegliere tra le due....
choose between the two

(vede sul tavolino alcuni ritratti in piccole
Sees *on the* *small table* *some* *portraits* *in* *small*

cornici.)
frames

--Forse questo è il loro ritratto. Carina questa
Maybe *this* *is* *-the-* *their* *portrait* *Carina* *this (one)*

col suo profilo greco, con que' capelli
with -the- *her* *profile* *greek,* *with* *that* *hair*

pettinati alla Niobe. Forse questa è il
combed *at the* *Niobe (style)* *Maybe* *this* *is* *the*

ventitrè.
(one that is) twenty-three

--Ma anche questo ventiquattro non c'è male.
But *also* *this* *twenty-four* *not* *-it- is* *bad*

Forse questa è bionda, e questa è bruna. Chi
Maybe *this (one)* *is* *blonde* *and* *this (one)* *is* *brunette* *Who*

mi consiglia? Il biondo è più romantico, più...
me *advises* *The* *blond* *is* *more* *romantic* *more*

simbolico... troppo Svezia e Norvegia. Il bruno
symbolic   too (much) Sweden and   Norway   The brunette

è quasi sempre segno di un carattere ardente,
is almost always sign of a character fiery

geloso... troppo Spagna e Portogallo. Che ti
jealous too (much) Spain and Portugal What you

dice il cuore, Nicolò? ventitrè o ventiquattro?...
says the heart Nicolo twenty-three or twenty-four

(pesa nelle mani i due ritratti.)
weighs in the hands the two portraits

--Sentiremo il consiglio della zia, che nella sua
(We) will listen to the advice of the aunt that in -the- her

esperienza saprà guidare un povero uomo sempre
experience will know to guide a poor man always

incerto nel cammino della vita.
incertain of the way of the life

(indicando un altro ritratto grande.)
indicating an other portrait large

--Certo questa vecchia cuffia è la zia dei buoni
Surely this old cap is the aunt of the good
(hag)

consigli. Lei conosce le due ragazze e saprà
advices She knows the two girls and will know

dirmi quale delle due ha più disposizioni al
to tell me which of the two has more dispositions to the

settimo sacramento. Per me capisco, che se
seventh sacrament For me (I) understand that if
{matrimony}

dovessi scegliere, farei la fine dell'asino
(I) had to choose (I) would make the end of the donkey
I would end up like the donkey

che, messo tra due fasci di fieno, si è
that put between two sheaves of hay himself is

lasciato morire di fame. Zitto, qualcun si avanza!
let to die of hunger Hush someone itself advances
is coming

(Si alza, fa una rapida toilette allo
Himself (he) rises makes a rapid toilet at the
He gets up (fix up)

specchio.)
mirror

--Forse   è   la   vecchia   zia.   Animo,   su,   coraggio.
Maybe   (it) is   the   old   aunt   Spirit   up   courage

Sei   stato   a   Custoza,   corpo   d'una   baionetta,   e
(You) are   been   at   Custoza   body   of a   bayonet   and
(You have)

devi   aver   paura   d'una   vecchia   cuffia?
(you) must   have   fear   of an   old   cap
(hag)

TERESITA
Teresita
{Little Theresa}

(una   vedovella   ancor   giovane,   simpatica,   vestita
A   little widow   still   young   sympathetic   dressed
(pretty widow)

con   finissima   semplicità   e   con   molto   buon   gusto.
with   very fine   simplicity   and   with   much   well   taste

Fa   un   inchino   a   Nicolò,   che   resta   un   istante
Makes   a   little bow   to   Nicolo   that   remains   (for) an   instant

imbarazzato.)
embarrassed

--Signore....
Mr.

NICOLÒ.
Nicolo

--Signora....
Mrs.

TERESITA.
Teresita

--Lei   ha   bisogno di parlarmi.
You   have   need   of   to talk to me

NICOLÒ.
Nicolo

--Sissignora...   cioè...   veramente   mia   sorella
Yes ma'am   that is   in truth   my   sister

Giacomina mi ha detto di chiedere della zia delle
Giacomina   me has said   to   ask   of the aunt of the

signorine, la vecchia zia, sissignora....
young ladies the   old   aunt   yes ma'am

TERESITA.
Little Theresa

--Sono io la zia delle signorine….
Am I the aunt of the misses
I am

NICOLÒ
Nicolo

(sorpreso.)
surprised

--Ah, lei fa da madre alle due orfanelle….
Ah you make of mother to the two little orphans
act as

(Avvicinandosi riconosce una antica amicizia.)
Approaching himself recognizes an old friendship

--Oh, ma scusi, noi ci conosciamo. Ah,
Oh but excuse (me) we each other know Ah

chi l'avrebbe detto dopo tanti anni? Lei, lei è
who it would have said after so many years She she is

la signora Teresita….
the Mrs. Teresita

TERESITA
Teresita

(fingendo di cader dalle nuvole.)
pretending of to fall from the clouds
        to be surprised

--E lei è il signor Nicolò.... Guarda che
And you are the Mr. Nicolo Look what

combinazione! ma si è fatto così grasso....
combination but yourself are gotten so fat
(a coincidence)

NICOLÒ
Nicolo

(ridendo con un po' di confusione.)
laughing with a bit of confusion

--Credevo che volesse dire: così vecchio!
(I) believe that (you) want to say so old

TERESITA
Teresita

(amabile.)
lovely

--Si è viaggiato insieme sulla strada della vita.
Oneself is traveled together on the path of -the- life

Guarda che combinazione!
See what combination
(a coincidence)

NICOLÒ.
Nicolo

--Guarda che combinazione!
Watch what combination
What a coincidence

(Segue un brevissimo imbarazzo d'ambo le parti.)
Follows a very brief embarrassment of both the parties

--Io credevo che la zia fosse una signora in età,
I believed that the aunt was a lady in age

colla cuffia.
with the cap

TERESITA.
Teresita

--La cuffia verrà... è in viaggio. Ma prego si
The cap will be (it) is in journey But please yourself

accomodi, signor Nicolò....
accommodate Mr. Nicolo

(Indica la sedia e siede lei per la prima.)
Notes the seat and sits herself for the first (time)

NICOLÒ
Nicolo

(ripetendo materialmente.)
repeating materially

--Guarda che combinazione....
Look at that combination
What a coincidence

(Prende la sedia, vi si appoggia, ma non
(He) takes the seat there himself leans but not

vi siede.
there sits

--Ma da quanto tempo non ci vediamo
But of how much time not each other (we) saw
(since)

più?
(any)more

TERESITA.
Teresita

--Oh è un gran pezzo! A che cosa devo
Oh (that) is a large piece At what thing must (I)
(stretch)

attribuire l'onore della sua visita?
attibute the honor of -the- your visit

NICOLÒ
Nicolo

(giocando colla sedia che fa girare sotto la
playing with the seat that (he) makes turn under the

mano.)
hand

--Mia sorella Giacomina mi ha detto: Va a
My sister Giacomina me has said Go to

Incirano, cerca della zia delle sorelle Bellini ed
Incirano close of the aunt of the sisters Bellini and

esponi il tuo caso.
pose -the- your case

TERESITA.
Teresita

--E qual è il suo caso?
And what is -the- your case

NICOLÒ.
Nicolo

--Il mio è un caso, dirò così, di coscienza:
The mine is a case (I) will say like this of conscience

ma ora non so se devo parlarne.
but now not (I) know if (I) must speak of it

TERESITA.
Teresita

--Perchè non deve parlarne?
Why not (you) must talk of it

NICOLÒ
Nicolo

(facendo girare più forte la sedia sotto la mano.)
making turn more strong the seat under the hand

--Perchè... io...
Because I

(dà   in una risata allegra)
(he) gives in   a   laugh   cheerful
(he utters)

--perchè io credevo che la zia fosse una cuffia....
because I believed that the aunt was   a   cap
                                              (old hag)

TERESITA
Teresita

(ride   anch'essa mentre   sì   abbandona nella
laughs   also she   while   herself abandons   in the

poltrona.)
armchair

--Dunque   è   alla cuffia che lei desidera parlare.
Then   (it) is to the cap that you desire   to talk
                         (old hag)   (would like)

NICOLÒ.
Nicolo

--No, stia buona, ora le   dirò   il   mìo caso.
No   stay well   now you (I) will tell -the- my   case

Ma è certo che, se avessi potuto immaginare di
But (it) is certain that if (I) had been able   to imagine   of

trovar qui lei al posto della... cuffia...
to find here you at the post of the cap
(hag)

(ride)
laughs

--non sarei venuto.
not (I) would be come
(I would have)

TERESITA
Teresita

(un po' offesa.)
a bit offended

--Non merito dunque la sua confidenza?
Not (I) merit therefore -the- your confidence

NICOLÒ.
Nicolo

--Lei merita tutto, ma il mio caso è di quelli
You merit all but -the- my case is of those

che hanno bisogno di molta indulgenza.
that have need of much indulgence

TERESITA.
Teresita

--Ma sieda….
But   sit

NICOLÒ
Nicolo

(mettendosi a sedere sull'angolo della sedia.)
setting himself to   sit   on the corner of the   chair

--Intanto mi dica: come   si   trova   qui a far
Meanwhile me tell   how   yourself (you) find here to make
                tell me

da madre a queste due bambine?
of mother to these two children

TERESITA.
Teresita

--Una serie di dolorose circostanze…. Oh sapesse
A   series of painful circumstances Oh   know

quante disgrazie! Morti i parenti di queste due
how many misfortunes Dead the parents of these two

povere figliuole, ho pensato ch'io potevo essere
poor daughters (I) have thought that I could be

utile in questa casa.
useful in this house

NICOLÒ
Nicolo

(esitando.)
hesitating

--Ma scusi. Lei non aveva sposato quel
But excuse (me) You not had married that

marchese?
marquis

TERESITA
Teresita

(molto riservata.)
very reserved

--Sì.
Yes

NICOLÒ
Nicolo

--E.... suo marito?
And   your husband

TERESITA.
Teresita

--È morto.
(He) is   dead

NICOLÒ
Nicolo

(con una certa sorpresa.)
with   a   certain   surprise

--Ah! è morto anche lui....
Ah   is dead   also   he

TERESITA.
Teresita

--In duello a Parigi.
In (a) duel at   Paris
            (in)

137

NICOLÒ.
Nicolo

--In duello a Parigi.... Guarda, guarda.
In   (a) duel at   Paris   See   see
         (in)

TERESITA
Teresita

(dopo un breve pensiero.)
after   a   short   thought

--Ma non parliamo dei morti. Quel che è
But   not   (we) talk   of the dead   That what is
                                                  (has)

passato, è passato.
passed   is passed
          (has)

NICOLÒ
Nicolo

(astratto in una sua idea.)
abstracted in -a- his   idea
(absorbed)

--O bello, o bello...
Oh   beautiful oh beautiful

TERESITA.
Teresita

--Che cosa?
What   thing

NICOLÒ
Nicolo

(si   corregge,   si   fa   serio,   si   alza.)
himself   corrects   himself makes serious himself   rises

--Mi rincresce di aver risvegliato delle dolorose
Myself   (I) regret   of to have   wakened   of the   painful

memorie.   Mi   scusi....
memories   Myself (I) excuse

(in atto di congedarsi)
in   act   of to say goodbye

--mi perdoni....
myself   (I) pardon

TERESITA
Teresita

(restando seduta.)
remaining seated

--Ma che cosa fa? lei non mi ha ancora detto
But what thing (you) do you not me have yet told
          are you doing

lo scopo della sua visita.
the scope of -the- your visit
    (purpose)

NICOLÒ.
  Nicolo

--È vero, ma io non so nemmeno se la mia
(That) is true but I not know even if -the- my

visita abbia uno scopo. Giacoraina
visit has a scope Giacoraina
        (purpose)

doveva avvertirmi di queste circostanze.
had to warn me of these circumstances
should have warned me

TERESITA
  Teresita

(con tono quasi materno.)
with (a) tone almost maternal

--Bene, si accomodi. Giacomina mi ha
Well   yourself accommodate   Giacomina   to me   has
accommodate yourself

scritto tutto. Lei e venuto a Incirano per uno
written   everything   You   are   come   to   Incirano   for   a
(have)

scopo molto lodevole e molto onesto. Vuol
purpose   very   commendable   and   very   honest   (You) want

prender moglie.
to take   (a) wife

NICOLÒ
Nicolo

(affettando una certa sicurezza.)
putting on   a   certain   assuredness

--Sì, voglio prender moglie.
Yes   (I) want   to take   (a) wife

TERESITA
Teresita

(ridendo con gaiezza simpatica.)
laughing   with   gayness   sympathetic

--O bello, o bello...
Oh   beautiful oh beautiful

NICOLÒ
Nicolo

(un po' mortificato.)
 a   bit   mortified

--Che cosa c'è di bello?
What   thing that is of beautiful

TERESITA.
Teresita

--Bello che il signor Nicolò voglia finalmente
Beautiful that the   Mr.   Nicolo   wants   finally

prender moglie.
 to take   (a) wife

(ride.)
laughs

NICOLÒ
Nicolo

(serio.)
serious

--Non rida o mi scoraggia.
(Do) not laugh or me discourage

TERESITA.
Teresita

--Ci ha pensato un pezzo il signor Nicolò.
There has thought a bit the Mr. Nicolo

NICOLÒ
Nicolo

(in tono di rimprovero.)
in (a) tone of reproach

--E di chi la colpa?
And of who the fault

TERESITA.
Teresita

--Di chi?
Of who

NICOLÒ.
Nicolo

--Ah Teresita! non si dovrebbero ricordare
Ah Teresita not yourself (you) should have remembered

certe cose....
certain things

(picchia nervosamente il bastoncino sul
(he) taps nervously the little (walking) stick on the

cappello.)
hat

TERESITA
Teresita

(gravemente.)
seriously

--Proprio!
Exactly

NICOLÒ.
Nicolo

--E tanto meno   si   dovrebbe ridere.
And   so   less yourself (you) should laugh

TERESITA
Teresita

(sospirando.)
sighing

--Si   ride quando si   è finito di piangere.
Oneself laughs when oneself is finished -of-   to cry
                            (has)

NICOLÒ
Nicolo

(con una punta d'ironia.)
with a   point of irony

--Beata lei che ha finito! Le donne son così facili
Blessed her that has finished The women are so simple

a dimenticare....
to   forget

TERESITA.
Teresita

--Si dimentica... per non odiare.
Oneself forgets for not to hate

NICOLÒ.
Nicolo

--Io non ho meritato il suo odio.
I not have merited -the- your hatred

(Con un leggero tono di sarcasmo.)
With a light tone of sarcasm

--A ogni modo la donna che sposava il marchese
At any way the woman that married the marquis
(case)

di San Luca deve aver trovato nel fasto del
of San Luca must have found in the pomp of -the-

suo blasone qualche conforto a' suoi dolori.
his coat of arms some comfort to her sorrows

TERESITA
Teresita

(offesa.)
offended

--Nicolò, non dite queste parole che offendono
Nicolo not say these words that offend

una donna che fu già troppo infelice nella sua
a woman that was already too unhappy in -the- her

vita. Voi sapete come sono andate le cose. Il
life You know how are went the things -The-
                        (have)

mio matrimonio fu per me una di quelle necessità
my matrimony was for me one of those necessities
    (marriage)

che il solo cuore d'una donna sa comprendere
that the sole heart of a woman knows to comprehend

e sa compatire. Voi sapete che mio padre
and knows to sympathize with You know that my father

era un uomo rovinato, che sulla nostra casa
was a man ruined that on -the- our house

stava il disonore e il fallimento, che soltanto
stood the dishonor and the failure that only
                        (bankruptcy)

un matrimonio di convenienza poteva salvare una
a marriage of convenience could save an

vecchia esistenza dalla disperazione. Allora voi
old existence from the despair Then you

eravate un giovine ufficiale senza fortuna,
were a young officer without fortune

nell'impossibilità di mettere una casa. Poi venne
in the impossibility of to put (up) a house Then came

la guerra e voi partiste per il campo....
the war and you left for the field (of battle)

NICOLÒ
Nicolo

(con amarezza.)
with bitterness

--E quando tornai dai pericoli della guerra,
And when (I) returned from the dangers of the war

seppi che Teresita Morando era diventata la
(I) found out that Teresita Morando was become the
(had)

marchesa di San Luca.
Marquise of San Luca

TERESITA
Teresita

(con un moto di ribellione.)
with a movement of rebellion

--Già, e non pensaste nemmeno ch'io
Already and not (you) thought even that I
(Yeah)

avessi potuto fare quel passo per un sentimento di
could taken do that step for a feeling of
could have taken

abnegazione e di dovere. Voi pensaste solamente
self-denial and of duty You thought only

e semplicemente che Teresita Morando, ragazza
and simply that Teresita Morando girl

vana, leggera, smaniosa di brillare, inebriata
vain light eager of to shine intoxicated
(flighty)

all'idea di portare una corona sul suo
at the idea of to wear a crown on -the- her

biglietto di visita, avesse dimenticato volontieri il
card of visiting had forgotten willingly the
business card

povero tenente per darsi nelle braccia di un
poor lieutenant for to give herself in the arms of an

vecchio nobile... sciupato dai piaceri. Questo
old nobleman worn from the pleasures This

solo voi avete pensato: e non sareste stato
only you had thought and not (you) would be been
(you) would have

un uomo se aveste pensato altrimenti. L'egoista
a man if (you) had thought otherwise The egoist

non è obbligato a compatire e meno a
not is obliged to pity and less to

comprendere... e tanto meno a perdonare.
understand and as less to pardon
(little)

NICOLÒ
Nicolo

(si alza, resta un istante come combattuto, e
Himself rises remains an instant like defeated and

mormora:)
murmurs

--Se sapeste invece quanto ha sofferto questo
If (you) knew instead how much has suffered this

egoista!
egoist

TERESITA
Teresita

(alzandosi anch'essa.)
Rising herself also that one

--E quest'ambiziosa oh! non ha forse sofferto! no.
And this ambitious one oh not has perhaps suffered no

Rapita dai bagliori de' suoi diamanti questa
Kidnapped of the gleams of -the- her diamonds this

vittima incoronata non ha versata mai una
victim crowned not has shed ever a

lagrima.... Nei tre anni del suo matrimonio
tear In the three years of -the- her marriage

con quell'infelice "boulevardier" essa passò di
with that miserable boulevard-walker that one passed from
(flaunter) (she)

trionfo in trionfo... invidiata da tutte le miserabili
triumph in triumph envied by all the miserables

che non hanno una corona sulla carrozza... e un
that not have a crown on the carriage and a

supplizio nel cuore.
torment in the heart

(Abbandonandosi alla sua passione.)
Abandoning herself at the her passion

--Voi non vi siete più occupato di me; ma
You not yourself are more occupied of me but
(have) cared for

per qualche motivo avete stentato a
for some motive (you) have found it hard to

riconoscermi. Voi avete trovato facilmente dei
recognize me You have found easily of the

dolci compensi...
sweet recompenses

(Arrestata improvvisamente da una specie di
Arrested suddenly by a kind of
(Halted)

rimorso, cangia tono, e con affettata naturalezza
remorse changes tone and with affection natural

ripiglia.)
again picks up
(continues again)

--Ma di che cosa si parla? oh buon Dio!
But from what thing -oneself- talks oh good God
we are talking

questo non è lo scopo della vostra visita. A
this not is the intent of -the- your visit For

che pro' disseppellire cose morte e finite?
what cause dig up things dead and finished

Sediamo: animo, sedetevi.... Veniamo all'argomento.
(We) sit soul sit down (We) come to the argument
(Let's sit) (Let's come)

(Come smarrita.)
As if lost

--Giacomina mi ha scritto.... Che cosa mi ha
Giacomina me has written What thing me has

scritto la buona amica? che voi volete
written the good friend that you want

accasarvi, che è tempo anche per voi di
to marry yourself that (it) is time also for you of

mettere giudizio. È giusto. Sa che le
to set judgment (It) is right (She) knows that the

povere mie nipoti son buone e brave ragazze
poor of mine nieces are good and fine girls

e anch'io sarei contenta di vederle collocate.
and also I would be happy of to see them placed

Ma sedetevi dunque, parlate.
But seat yourself then talk

NICOLÒ
Nicolo

(con espressione patetica.)
with expression pathetic

--No, no, non ho più nulla a dire. Scusate,
No no not (I) have more nothing to say Excuse (me)

Teresita, io non son più degno di accostarmi a
Teresita I not am more worthy of to accost myself to

una donna....
   a   woman

(Si   ritira   qualche passo per andar via.)
Himself retires   some   step   for to go away
       (draws back)

TERESITA.
  Teresita

--Non andate in collera per quello che vi   ho
Not   go   in anger for   that   what you (I) have

detto. Vi domando scusa se vi   ho   offeso.
said You (I) ask   pardon if you (I) have offended

 Sedetevi,   ragioniamo.   Accettate   almeno   un
Seat yourself let's discuss   Accept   at least   a

bicchierino di vermouth....
 shot (glass) of   vermouth

(Toglie   da uno stipo una bottiglia di cristallo
(She) takes from a cabinet a   bottle of   glass

 e offre un bicchierino a Nicolò.)
and offers a   shot   to Nicolo

NICOLÒ
Nicolo

(sforzandosi a rifiutare.)
forcing himself to   refuse
  (trying)

--No, no, lasciatemi andare. Non merito   più
No   no   let me   go   Not   (I) merit (any)more

nulla. La mia vita è finita da un pezzo.
nothing -The- my life is finished from a   piece
                                      long ago

TERESITA.
Teresita

--Devo   proprio mettermi una vecchia cuffia in
(I) must   myself   set me   an   old   cap   in

testa   per persuadervi a ragionare?
(the) head for to persuade you to   reason
                                      (talk)

(Nicolò accetta il bicchierino.)
Nicolo   accepts the   shot

--Se vi   ho   offeso perdonatemi. Voi avete per
If   you (I) have offended pardon me   You   have   by

errore messa una punta di ferro sopra una
mistake put a point of iron on a

cicatrice e io ho gridato di dolore. Ma ora è
scar and I have screamed of pain But now (it) is

passato. Qua....
passed Here

(Lo fa sedere e siede anche lei.)
It makes to sit and sits also she

--Posso aiutarvi, voglio consigliarvi, perchè in
(I) can help you (I) want to advise you because in

fondo ho molta stima di voi.
(the) bottom (I) have much esteem of yo
(for)

NICOLÒ.
Nicolo

--Io invece non ho nessuna stima di me. Io ho
I instead not have none at all esteem of me I have
(for)

sempre creduto che non valesse la pena di
always believed that not (it) is worth the trouble of

voler bene a una donna. Ho atrocemente
to want well to a woman (I) have atrociously

sofferto, ma non per pietà della vittima
suffered but not for pity of the victim
(out of)

inghirlandata. Ho sofferto solamente per il
garlanded (I) have suffered only for -the-

mio orgoglio ferito. Avete detto bene poco fa.
my pride hurt (You) have said well a little makes
just now

Il mio nome è Egoista. Quando un uomo non è
-The- my name is Egoist When a man not is

capace di comprendere, di compatire, di
capable -of- to understand -of- to sympathize -of-

perdonare, non merita più che una donna
to forgive not (he) merits (any)more that a woman

gli voglia bene....
him wants well

(Volta via la faccia alquanto commosso, tracanna
Turns away the face rather moved gulps down

d'un fiato il bicchierino, va a collocarlo sullo
of a breath the shot goes to place it on the
(with a)

stipo, e si prepara a congedarsi.)
cabinet and himself prepares to take leave himself
(leave)

TERESITA
Teresita

(si alza, un po' soprapensiero.)
Herself rises a bit thoughtful

--Permetta che le presenti almeno le bambine.
Permit (me) that you (I) present at least the children

Per quanto senza cuffia so esercitare i doveri
For as much without cap (I) know to exercise the duties

dell'ospitalità.
of -the- hospitality

(Dal giardino risona un campanello.)
From the garden sounds a bell

--Ecco, son le ragazze che tornano colla
See are the girls that return with the

governante.
> matron

NICOLÒ
> Nicolo

(cercando di sfuggire.)
> searching -of- to flee
> (trying)

--No, no, non voglio veder nessuno; non voglio
> No no not (I) want to see no one not (I) want

lasciarmi vedere.
> to let me see

TERESITA.
> Teresita

--Mettiamoci qui, dietro a questo paravento. Da
> (We) set you here behind to this screen From

qui possiamo vederle senza essere veduti.
> here (we) can see them without to be seen

(Conduce Nicolò per mano fin presso la porta
> Leads Nicolo by (the) hand until close (to) the door

dietro un paravento e indica le ragazze che
behind a screen and indicates the girls that

passano in giardino.)
pass in (the) garden

--Guardi la prima, la bionda, ha ventidue
Look at the first the blond (she) has twenty-two
(she is)

anni, è un angiolino di bontà, piena di
years (she) is an angel of goodness full of

sentimento. L'altra, la bruna, Annetta, è un
feeling The other the brunette Annetta is a

carattere più serio, ha molto ingegno, conosce
character more serious has much talent knows

molto bene la musica....
very well the music

(Nicolò, stringendo la mano di Teresita, trascinato
Nicolo squeezing the hand of Teresita pulled

dalla forza dell'antica passione, posa un bacio sui
of the force of the old passion poses a kiss on the
(by the)

capelli di lei e resta come fulminato dalla
hairs of her and remains as (though) struck of -the-
(hair)

sua stessa audacia.)
his own audacity

(Teresita, sfuggendogli, dice con accento di
Teresita fleeing him says with accent of
on a tone

profondo rimprovero, ma senza ira:)
profound reproach but without anger

--Che cosa fa, Nicolò....
What thing (you) do Nicolo
What are you doing

(va a sedersi e nasconde la faccia nelle mani.)
goes to seat herself and hides the face in the hands

NICOLÒ
Nicolo

(dopo essere rimasto un gran pezzo come
after to be remained a large stretch like

trasognato, si accosta pianino a Teresita e
dreamy himself approaches quietly to Teresita and

con voce sommessa piena di note tenere e
with voice soft full of notes tender and

appassionate, dice, quasi curvo su di lei:)
passionate says almost bent over -of- her

--Io non ho conosciuto che una donna nella
I not have known that one woman in the
(other than)

mia vita e basta! la bionda, la bruna, la
my life and enough the blond the brunette the

sentimentale e la donna assennata, tutte le
sentimental and the woman sensible all the

bontà e tutte le bellezze di una creatura di
goodness and all the beauties of a creature of

donna son già passate nel mio cuore il
woman are already passed in -the- my heart the

giorno che vi siete passata voi, Teresita. Voi vi
day that there are passed you Teresita You there
(have)

avete lasciato un modello così sublime, che, al
have left a model so sublime that at the

confronto, tutte le altre mi sembrano immagini
comparison all the others me seem images

sbiadite. Chi ama bene una volta ha amato per
faded Who loves well one time has loved for

sempre. Il destino non ha voluto che voi foste
ever The destiny not has wanted that you were

mia, e "amen"! È bene che io non guasti il
mine and amen (It) is well that I not waste -the-

mio ideale. Se Giacomina non mi avesse cacciato
my ideal If Giacomina not me had chased

qui, io non sarei venuto mai a questa ricerca di
here I not would be come ever to this research of

commesso viaggiatore. È peccato sciupare
commissioned traveler (It) is sin to spoil

l'amore vivo con degli amori artificiali; non
the love living with of the loves artificial not

barattiamo l'oro colla carta.... Addio.
trade the gold with the paper Goodbye

TERESITA
Teresita

(non contenta.)
not   happy

--Che dovrò scrivere dunque a Giacomina?
What   will (I) have to   write   then   to   Giacomina

Che abbiamo fatto fiasco?
That   (we) have   made   failure
          failed

NICOLÒ.
Nicolo

--Le scriverò io, se permettete. Siccome non
Her   will write   I   if   you allow (it)   Since   not

tornerò a casa sua prima della fin del mese
(I) will return   to   house   her   before   of the   end   of the   month

e forse più tardi, è bene che le mandi due
and   maybe   more   late   (it) is   well   that   her   (I) send   two

righe. Se mi favorite carta e penna.
lines   If   me   (you) favor   card   and   pen
         (you can give)

TERESITA
Teresita

(preparando le cose su un altro tavolino.)
Preparing   the things on an other small table

--Intendete viaggiare?
Do (you) intend   to travel

NICOLÒ
Nicolo

(siede al tavolino e prende la penna.)
Sits   at the small table and takes the   pen

--Sì, ho bisogno di cambiar aria. Son mezzo
Yes (I) have need of to change air (I) am half

malato, mi sento vecchio e malinconico. Andrò
sick   me (I) feel old   and melancholy (I) will go

a Parigi anch'io in cerca di distrazione.
to Paris also I in search of distraction

(scrive:)
writes

--"Cara Giacomina...."
Dear Giacomina

TERESITA
Teresita

(seduta in disparte ha preso in mano un
seated -in- apart has taken in (the) hand a

lavoruccio.)
handiwork
(small sewing job)

--Parigi non è una città troppo indicata per della
Paris not is a city too (well) suited for -of the-

gente ammalata. Voi avete bisogno d'una buona
people sick You have need -of- a good

infermiera.
nurse

NICOLÒ.
Nicolo

--"Cara Giacomina...." Aiutatemi a scrivere questa
Dear Giacomina Help me to write this

lettera....
letter

TERESITA
Teresita

(con   energia,   dopo   aver   buttato   via   il
with   energy   after   to have   thrown   away   the

lavoro.)
work
(small sewing job)

--Sì,   scrivete   sotto   dettatura: --Cara   Giacomina,
Yes   write   under   dictation   Dear   Giacomina

siccome io sono... un uomo di poca fede....
since   I   am   a   man   of   little   faith

(Nicolò scrive sotto dettatura: qui s'interrompe.)
Nicolo   writes   under   dictation   here   himself interrupts
(he stops)

TERESITA
Teresita

.

(comandando.)
commanding

--Scrivete, animo! "Son destinato a soffrir sempre
Write   spirit   Am   destined   to   suffer   always
C'mon write

per non conchiudere mai nulla." Avete scritto?
for   not   to conclude   ever   nothing   (You) have   written (it)
never anything

(Si alza e passeggia un po' nervosa.)
Herself   rises   and   walks around   a   little   nervous

NICOLÒ
Nicolo

(scrive.)
writes

--"Mai nulla".... Ho scritto.
Ever   nothing
never anything

TERESITA.
Teresita

--Punto e a capo. "Io non credo nella virtù
Point   and   at   head   I   not   believe   in the   virtue
(end)

della donna....
of the   woman
of women

NICOLÒ.
Nicolo

--Scusate....
Excuse you
(Excuse me)

TERESITA
Teresita

(lasciandosi sempre più trasportare dalla passione.)
letting herself always more transport of the passion
(rouse)

--No, no. Dovete scrivere la vostra condanna.
No no (You) must write -the- your condemnation
(sentence)

"Non credo... che una donna...
Not (I) believe that a woman

possa aver conservato puro il suo ideale...
can have conserved pure -the- her ideal
may have kept

mentre....
while

(parlando direttamente a Nicolò che lascia cadere
talking directly to Nicolo that lets fall
(who)

la   penna.)
the   pen

--mentre intorno a lei   si   commerciavano gli
while   around   to her themselves   traded   the
were traded out

affetti   e   si   commettevano le più ignobili
affections and themselves   committed   the most ignoble
(vile)

vigliaccherie. Non   credo   che una donna possa
cowardices   Not   (I) believe that a   woman   can

sopravvivere   al   suo stesso dolore   e   alle
survive   -to the- her own   pain and -to the-

sue   umiliazioni: non   credo   che
her   humiliations   not   (I) believe   that

possa ancora conservare intatto il tesoro de' suoi
can   still   conserve   intact   the treasure of   her
she may still keep

affetti   e   possa compensare un uomo di
affections and can   compensate a   man   of
(for)

averla amata bene una volta....
to have her loved   well one   time

171

NICOLÒ
Nicolo

(afferra le mani di Teresita, le porta alla bocca,
Grabs the hands of Teresita them carries to the mouth

inginocchiato davanti a lei.)
kneeling in front to her
(of)

--Dunque tu mi ami ancora?
Then you me love still

TERESITA
Teresita

(svegliandosi da una specie di sogno.)
waking herself from a kind of dream
(waking up) (some)

--Che fate? io non parlavo di me. Scrivete.
What do (you) I not talked of me Write
(are you doing)

NICOLÒ.
Nicolo

--Donna di poca fede, perchè ingannarci ancora?
Woman of little faith why deceive us still

TERESITA.
Teresita

--Io parlavo di queste povere ragazze orfane.
I talked of these poor girls orphan
orphan girls

NICOLÒ.
Nicolo

--Esse hanno bisogno di un padre. Scrivete voi,
Those have need of a father Write you
You write

detterò io....
will say I
I will dictate

(La fa sedere al suo posto.)
Her makes sit at the his place

TERESITA
Teresita

(resistendo.)
Resisting

--Nicolò, che cosa ho detto? io provo un
Nicolo what thing have (I) said I feel a
what did I say

rimorso.... Voi non siete venuto per me.
remorse You not were come for me
you did not come

NICOLÒ.
Nicolo

--Scrivete "Cara Giacomina"....
Write Dear Giacomina

(Teresita si sforza a scrivere.)
Teresita herself forces to write

(Nicolò detta:)
Nicolo says

--Ni... co... lò mi a... ma; --punto e virgola.
Ni... co... lo me lo... ves point and comma
{Nicolo} {Nicolo}{Nicolo} {loves}{loves} semicolon

--Io a... mo Nicolò. Dunque t... o...
I lo... ve Nicolo Then t... o...
{love}{love} {latin: (that's) all}{latin: (that's) all}

to. E Teresita non dice di no. E la
to And Teresita not says -of- no And the
{latin: (that's) all}

cara zietta, senza la cuffietta, si lascierà
dear auntie without the bonnet herself lets

finalmente baciare la bocca da un vecchio ragazzo
finally — kiss the mouth by an old boy

che l'ama da dieci anni.
that her loves from ten years
(since)

TERESITA.
Teresita

--Odiandola....
Hating her

NICOLÒ.
Nicolo

--Sì. L'amore perchè resista al tempo bisogna
Yes The love however resists to the time needs

come l'oro mescolarlo in una piccola lega d'odio
like the gold to mix it in a little alloy of hate

e di gelosia. Sì, io ti ho odiata, ti odio...
and of jealousy Yes I you have hated you hate

perchè ti amo.
because you (I) love

TERESITA.
Teresita

--Zitto, le ragazze....
Hush the girls

(Si alza un po' spaurita e con voce
Herself rises a bit frightened and with voice

supplichevole soggiunge:)
imploring (she) adds

--E andrete proprio via?
And (you) go right away

NICOLÒ.
Nicolo

--Sicuro, bisogna che io corra ad avvertire
Sure (it is) necessary that I run to warn

Giacomina di queste novità. Ve la manderò
Giacomina of these news (To) you her (I) will order
(this)

qui.
here

TERESITA.
Teresita

--Qui no: ci son troppe ragazze. Andrò io da
Here no here are too (many) girls Will go I of
(to)

lei. Mio Dio! e che diranno queste povere
her My God and what will say these poor

figliuole? io che dovrei pensare al loro destino,
daughters I that should think at -the- their destiny
(future)

e invece.... Bella zia che sono! ma non sono
and instead Beautiful aunt that (I) am but not (I) am
(Nice) (have I)

invecchiata, Nicolò?
aged Nicolo

(Va a guardarsi nello specchio.)
Goes to look at herself in the mirror

--Non sono magra e distrutta dal dolore? Non
Not (I) am thin and destroyed of the pain Not

merito proprio una cuffia? Che cosa dirà il
(I) merit myself a bonnet What thing will say the

mondo?
world

NICOLÒ
Nicolo

(ridendo mentre passa il braccio nel braccio
laughing while (he) passes the arm in the arm

di lei.)
of her

--Il mondo dirà che amor vecchio non invecchia:
The world will say that love old not ages

e che il miglior modo per prender moglie è...
and that the best way -for- to take (a) wife is

di parlarne alla zia.
-of- to talk of it to the aunt